GINA SCHOOL

Gina Barreca

artwork by John Guillemette

woodhall press

Norwalk, CT

woodhall press

Woodhall Press, Norwalk, CT 06855
WoodhallPress.com

Cover design and layout: John Guillemette

Library of Congress Cataloging-in-Publication Data available

ISBN 978-1-960456-41-0 (paper: alk paper)
ISBN 978-1-960456-42-7 (electronic)

First Edition
Distributed by Independent Publishers Group
(800) 888-4741

Printed in the United States of America

GINA SCHOOL is
dedicated to Becca and
Zach, who inspired the
collection.

GINA SCHOOL: AN INTRODUCTION
(NOT TO BE CONFUSED WITH OUR ADMISSIONS BROCHURE)

This introduction came easy—I'm simply doing what I've done since that glorious day when I could afford the co-pay for therapy: I'm attempting to provide an origin story and a justification for existence. The passages here grow from experiences and ideas planted long ago and, like invitations chalked on handmade signs along rural routes during times of harvest, I invite you to pick your own. (Personally, I don't go outdoors and rarely walk on unpaved surfaces if I can help it, but I have seen those signs. Or photographs of them.)

Possessing a delightful (some would say enthralling) habit of knowing precisely what people need to hear, it's virtually imperative for me to dispense wisdom. It's almost a vice, really, but with all the good I've done in the world, nobody could say that (at least not to my face and not more than once). It's hard to control the urge to shout advice at unsuspecting schmoes.

In the public restroom shared by students and faculty at the university where I teach, I noticed recently that in the stall next to mine a young woman had pooled her clothes—a pair of cheerfully embroidered denim overalls—on the floor next to her feet.

As a person who, in her youth, also wore overalls, I know that one of the great inconveniences of that fashion choice is the impossibility of using the bathroom without removing your entire outfit. But as an adult, it took all my inner strength not to yell, "For heaven's sake, kid, get your clean clothes off the toilet floor!"

That young person needed Gina School. Many do in a world where taking a lot of selfies passes for leading an examined life.

The concept of Gina School was inspired by a conversation with another young woman, the daughter of one of my best friends. We were at an elegant dinner celebrating her parents' marriage anniversary. I was seated next to this daughter and her long-term boyfriend.

A man of good character and steady habits, the 24-year-old

nevertheless lacked certain graces. Our dinner hosts had carefully chosen the dishes to be served, having addressed in advance the dietary needs of over 20 guests from four countries. In their magnanimity, they had also choreographed a selection of wines to accompany each course. For non-drinkers, there was sparkling water. A detailed menu, printed on deliciously creamy paper, explained what we would be served.

When asked which wine he would like with his appetizer, the nice young man rather grandly ordered a gin and tonic. He shrugged, "What can I say? I'm not a wine guy."

His girlfriend made a small face, like a fastidious cat catching the scent of a lemon peel.

Having worked with young people for the last 40 years of my life, I instructed with no hesitation, "Then have water. Do not make the servers schlep all the way to the bar in a different part of the restaurant to fetch you gin when nobody offered it to you and nobody else is having it."

His girlfriend, leaning over him to address me, said, "Can he attend Gina School?"

Even Mr. Gin and Tonic thought Gina School was a good idea. (He canceled his drink order that evening and had a small wine. Several years have passed, and the two young people are now happily married to one another. This book is dedicated to them.)

This tidy volume is a cross between a medieval Book of Hours one might find in the Special Collections at the University of Cambridge and a pile of notes written on the back of Erma Bombeck's shopping receipts. Gina School functions like a manuscript of instructions culled from Ann Landers, Virginia Woolf, Dorothy Parker, and ELLE Magazine meticulously illuminated by the reincarnation of a monk obsessed with appropriate marginalia.

To make Gina School meaningful, memorable, and manifest, I had the wisdom to ask John Guillemette to illustrate the passages. I knew John was talented, but he gave new dimensions to the language in ways that startled and delighted me. The book became multi-dimensional; we saw around, above, behind, and beneath the words. (John is no medieval monk, by the way, but a promising writer and accomplished former student born long after I stopped listening to popular music.)

Gina School accepts early admissions, mature students, speed readers, auditors, book groups, gloriously erudite librarians, anxious applicants in need of reassurance, slow readers, and writers in need of prompts. Also accepted are harsh critics who pay full price. Scholarships are available to those who buy in bulk.

Before you enter the world of image, here are some Gina School basics:

1. Replacing recklessness with self-reliance is the definition of being a grown-up.

2. Learn the names of everybody you deal with on a regular basis. These include, but are not limited to, the names of your friends' children and grandchildren (and pets, excluding fish). Be able to greet by name, if possible, the cashiers, bus drivers, delivery people, caretakers, bartenders, servers, postal carriers, teachers, and corrections officers you see frequently. Saying "I'm no good with names" is a lazy way of excusing yourself from believing that other people are important. Other people are important. To most of the world, you are other people.

3. If you suspect somebody might need help, offer it. The worst that'll happen is you'll be shooed away because the situation is under control. But you might also be able to make a significant change in someone's day. Offer directions—if you know your way around, that is. Offer to take a photo of a big group if you see that one of them is being left out of the picture. If you see an item drop out of somebody's bag or pocket, let them know.

4. Clean up after yourself. You ate from it, cooked with it, slept in it, depleted it? Don't just leave it there for somebody else. Wash it. Replace it. The world is not your mother, and even your mother is getting tired of this stuff.

5. The easiest thing in the world is to make somebody else miserable; it doesn't take talent, wit, insight or guts to inflict emotional harm. Anybody can do it. Notice that for many people, making others miserable is not only their hobby, but their singular art form. To make another person feel significant, recognized, cherished, or admired, however, is a challenge that only a generous and self-respecting human being can accept.

6. Learn to address an envelope by hand and learn how to use a stamp. Then go to the post office and mail your handwritten thank-you letters in a timely fashion.

7. Avoid clichés, such as "in a timely fashion" whenever possible, but don't lose sleep (sic) over them.

8. There are people who treat stepping out in front of moving cars as a dare. Their contempt for anyone gauche enough to drive while they're walking is as obvious as their noise-cancelling headphones, sunglasses, and cellphones (which they scroll through as they wander the streets). We're not doing those very basic things we were taught when we were little— we're not watching out, we're not looking both ways, we're not alert to what's going on. Enclosed in an increasingly personal space, we have less engagement in the world itself. After all, if we're not noticing oncoming cars, we're not noticing when green trees become tinged with gold and red; we don't see the wild geese, or tiny chipmunks who have mastered the art of dodging traffic. We might miss the smile tossed our way—one we might've caught in one of those thrilling, unscripted, chance connections between human beings. There's a lot to miss if you don't look up. If you're on automatic all the time, then you really are crossing roads just to get to the other side.

9. There are no quizzes in Gina School. There is no final grade. It's an open-book platform and taking notes on every page is encouraged; so is coloring and so is adding your own art. The only requirement is to keep going with bravery, curiosity, and a sense of personal achievement. Don't let your plans or fears for the future eclipse your experience of today.

10. Pick everything up off the floor, kid, and pay attention.

1

YOU CAN SAY
ANYTHING
YOU
WANT

but watch your tone. If you can make "Pass the salt" sound like "I adore you," then you're in good shape. If you make "How are you today?" sound like "Drop dead" you might need more practice.

DON'T MISTAKE

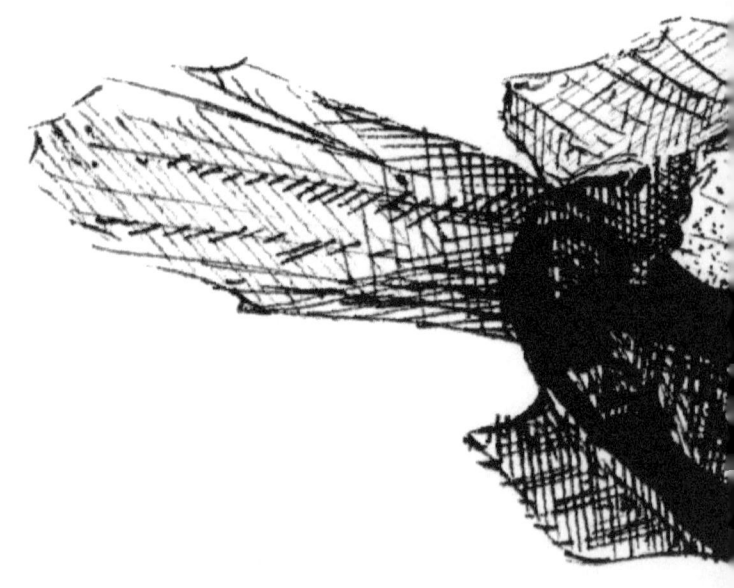

words for truth. Don't
assume what you hear is
what was meant.

2

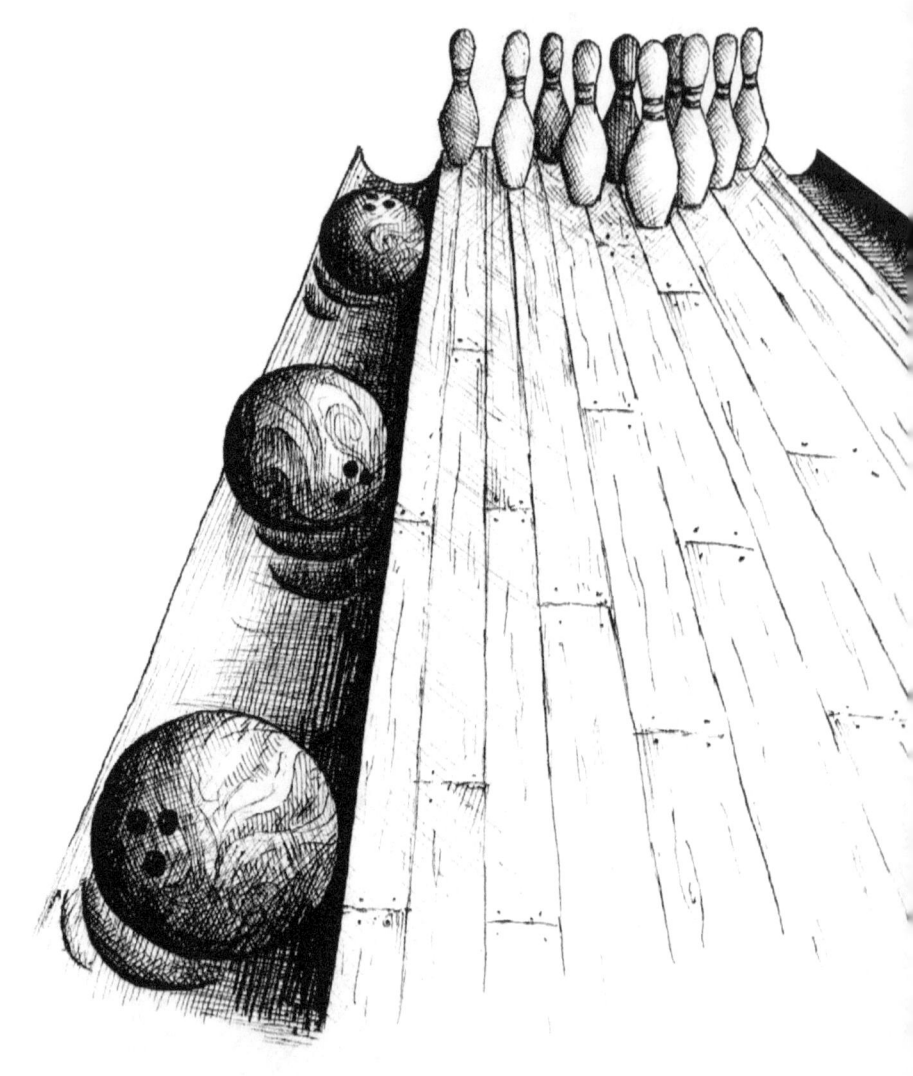

AVOID BEING ONE
OF THE PEOPLE

who believes the only way to
make up for doing something
wrong is to keep doing it.

YOUNG FRIEND:

"We're going to
visit my husband's
parents. During
part of it, we're
doing an escape
room adventure."

MICHAEL:

"What's that?"

YOUNG FRIEND:

"It's where a group of people who don't really know each other are locked in together and need to figure out how to get out within a set time limit."

MICHAEL:

"Basically a regular family holiday, then."

FIRST LOVES

are adorable.
Last loves are
magnificent.

6

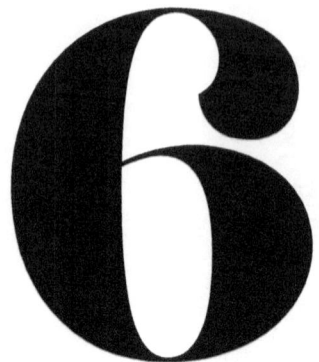

EVERY
DAY

has its own continental divide: certain hours flow toward the morning and others go toward the night, just as, after a certain point in your life, there are years which connect you back to your youth while others move you along towards your death. Remember to change the clocks, doll.

THE
POINT OF
THE TASK

is not to finish it but to start it; don't worry yet about how it will end. If you hesitate to begin because you are afraid that you won't be able to complete it, you are doing the very thing guaranteeing that outcome.

SKIN PRODUCTS

containing 24-karat gold extract might
just come in handy—if financial times
get really tough. You could, in a pinch,
always pawn your own head.

9

WHEN
RELATIONSHIPS
END

in the worst way, you
wreck the inside of
somebody, overturn
the flimsy altars in
the sanctuary of
themselves.

THOSE BORN
INTO MONEY

—not necessarily the irrefutably rich, but the socially and culturally privileged—have a distinct way of handling the world, as if simply overseeing what belongs to them.

(...)

(Life reveals most
significant truths
parenthetically.)

I
LIVE
THE
EDGY
LIFE

of someone who has no idea
whether it's a check number, a check
amount, or simply an interesting
historical date when I see "1206" on a
slip of paper next to my checkbook.
Don't be like me.

12

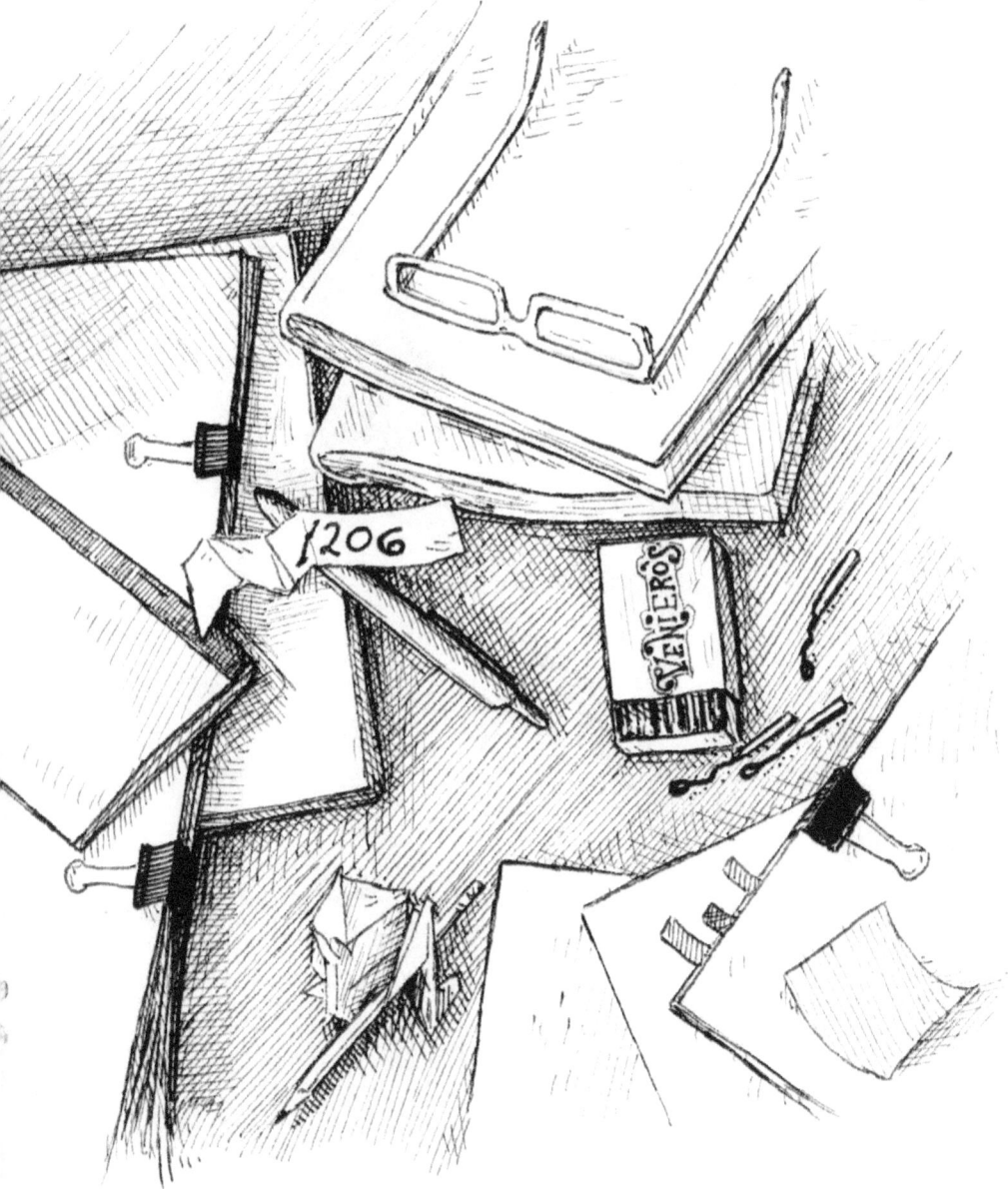

FOR ITALIANS,

13

cooking is more
choreography than
culinary.

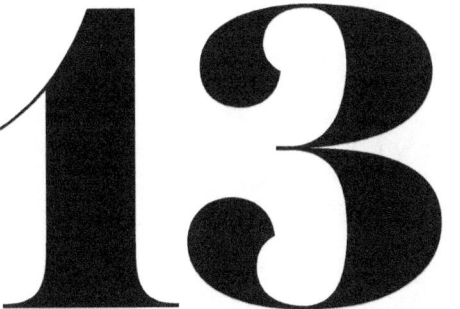

ONE OF
THE GREATEST
ILLUSIONS

in life is that, someday, you'll know better. I
hate to break it to you, but it's not something
that happens automatically. Wisdom is not like
getting your period or going bald or having
to procure a product that helps you with acid
reflux: it's not something that happens with age.

15

IF YOU KNOW

you can do it—if you can already chart
every day in your future—then why
bother? Choose to do something you
have more trouble imagining.

Take a chance.

HOW DO YOU KNOW

16

WHEN IT'S OVER?

You no longer wonder if it's over.

AS WE CHANGE, LOVE CHANGES.

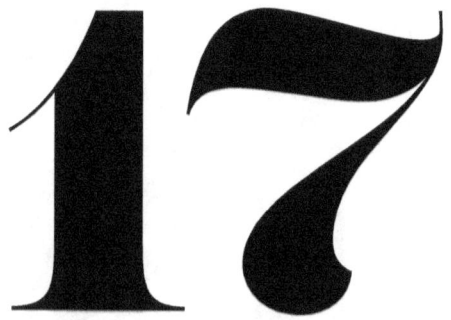

As a youth, you fall for an unattainable ideal. When you're more mature, you fall in love with a person: "Sure, he has only one eye in the middle of his forehead," you'll rationalize, "but he never forgets my birthday."

BEACH DAY!!

DON'T HOPE FOR
A FAST ANSWER.

Hope for the right answer.

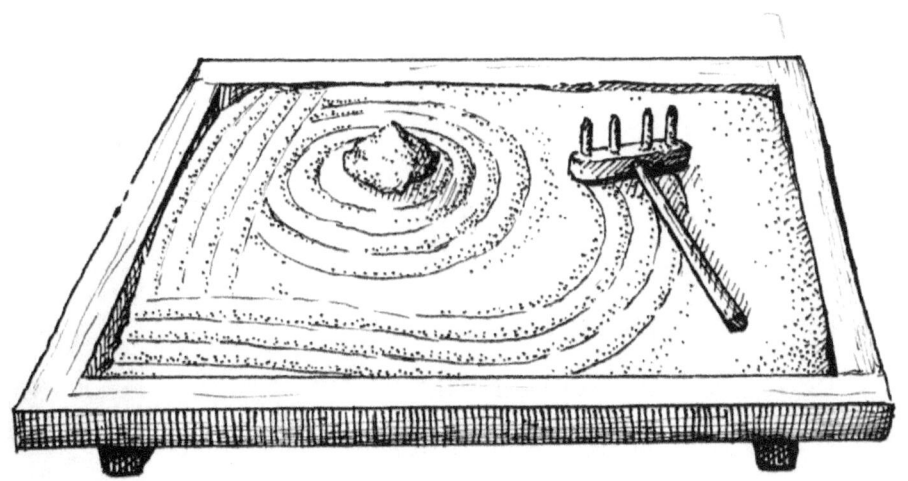

WOMEN HAVE

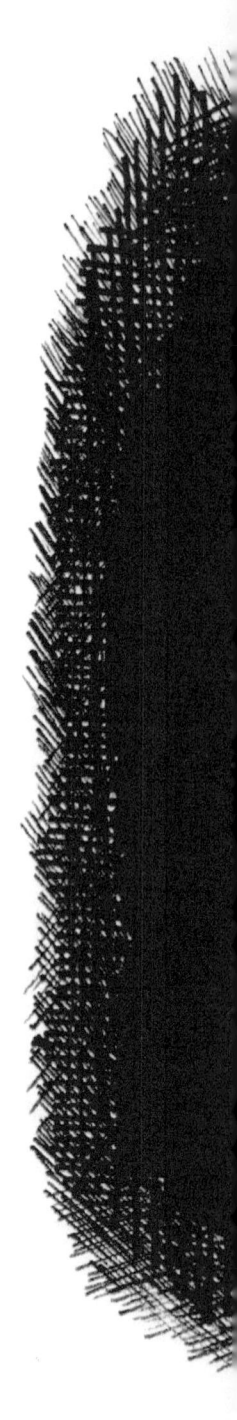

at least one version of ourselves
packed away in a suitcase under
the bed. She's an escape route.
She's another edition, not quite
a duplicate, maybe our self from
another life. Like the moon, our
unknown selves shift and tug at
us, exerting forces both profound
and unacknowledged.

I LIVE FOR SCRAPS.

I want the bits: the burnt parts, the crispiest pieces, the gravy, and the bones. When Springsteen sings that "spare parts and broken hearts" keep the world turning? He's right. Leftovers are not only the best part of Thanksgiving; for many of us, leftovers are the best parts of life.

AUTHENTIC

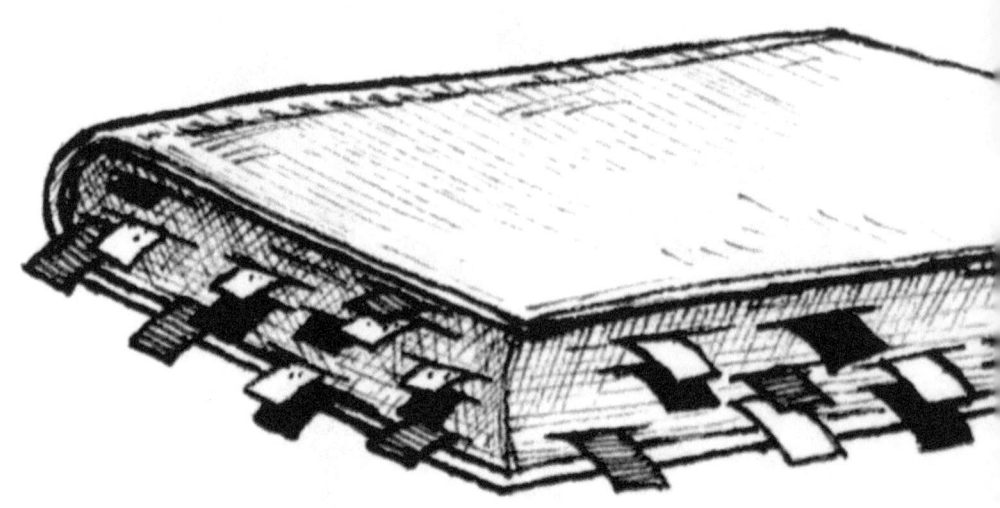

EDUCATION

demands that students learn, and not merely that they are taught. It's not about simply offering access to information or data. What happens in classrooms is not the same as what happens at UPS: it is not like transferring an unexamined parcel of information from one person to another. It must include, as all reputable teachers know, instructing students in academic discipline and personal responsibility.

EVERY
YOUNG
PERSON

22

should have a job for an extended period of time where they need to show up on time, in clean clothes, fully sober, wide-awake, in a convincingly cheerful mood. Work matters. Having a job matters.

23

WORK
MATTERS.

But it's not always rewarded. There are
people who labor their whole lives but are
never rewarded with success. Not every dog
has its day; some simply work their tails off.

LEARN TO PLAY
TO A TOUGH
CROWD...

...AT AN EARLY AGE.

True story: At age six or so, after watching an old Broadway musical on *Million Dollar Movie* and imitating one of the stars, I yelled, "I wanna see my name up in lights!" My Uncle Bill, without missing a beat, said "So change your name to 'Vacancy'." I wasn't even sure what the joke meant, but the rest of the family was hysterical. (From Uncle Bill, I learned the importance of getting the last laugh.)

25 "GROW

where you are planted," applies only to vegetable matter. What are you, an endive? Shake off the dust. Move around.

HUMOR IS ALCHEMY.

26

Transforming a crisis, insecurity, or tragedy
into comedy confers a validity on a life
otherwise denied value or meaning.

DO UNTO YOURSELF AS YOU

Start treating yourself with as much generosity, charity, kindness, and graciousness as you would treat the least favorite among your acquaintances. Be as kind and as forgiving toward yourself as you would be toward a pal. Stop torturing yourself about what you might have done (or not done) 10 days ago or 10 years ago. Offer comfort to yourself that actually helps, such as cleaning out old wounds and cleaning up old messes.

WOULD DO UNTO OTHERS.

27

Don't rely on merely short-term diversions, such as drinking heavily before lunch or eating an entire Sara Lee cheesecake before letting it defrost. You wouldn't suggest to a friend that she do such things; why allow yourself to do them? Imagine you're put in charge of taking care of yourself the way you might be privileged to take care of someone you love.
Then do it.

PUT, ON A PAGE,

one word after another. Then
you can edit. Then you can
decide if it works. Stop writing
in your head. Stop doing
research. And for the love of
gawd, stop talking about it.

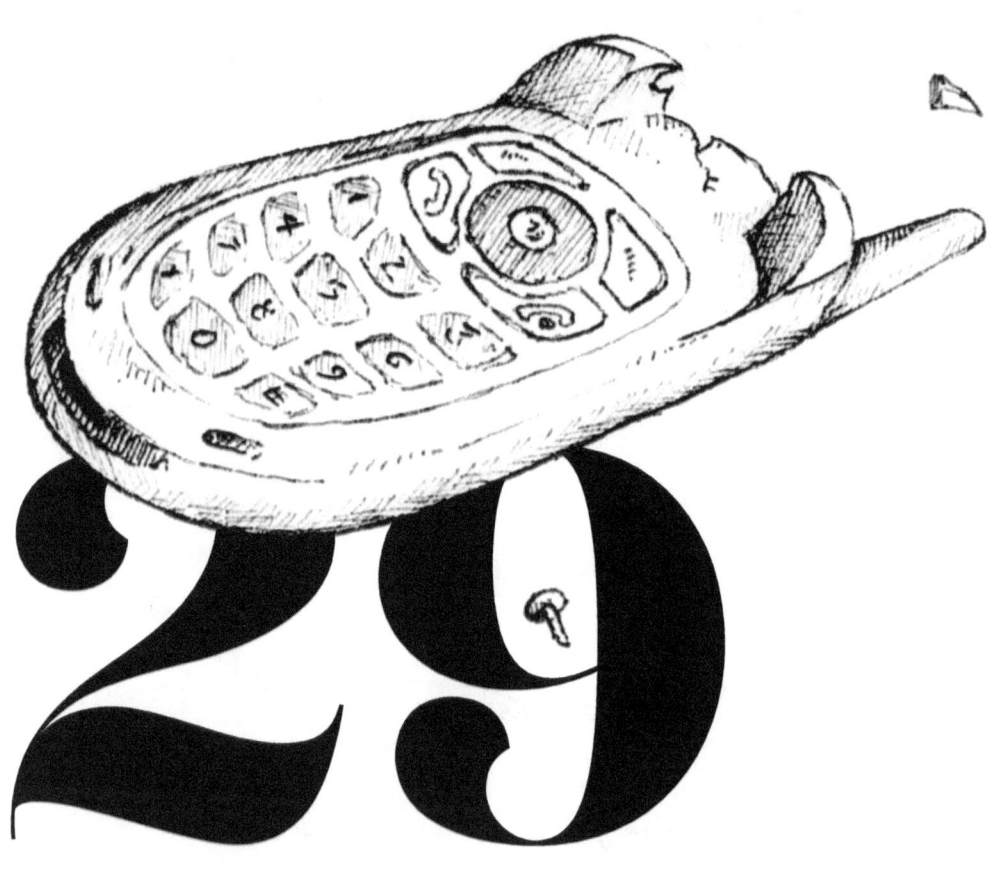

DON'T ASK

questions if you're unwilling
to deal with the answers.

Truth takes courage to hear
as well as to speak.

ALL SORTS OF

30

have encouraged us to sit politely and wait to be chosen. Remember the game "Duck, Duck, Goose," where you sat in a circle facing the center and waited to be recognized as the "goose," whereupon you were tapped and permitted to run around making choices yourself? And how many fairy tales taught us essentially the same lesson? "Duck, Duck, Cinderella!" "Duck, Duck, Snow White!" Or classic novels? "Duck, Duck, Madame Bovary!" "Duck, Duck, Anna Karenina!" Does sitting pretty turn you into a sitting duck?

LESSONS

ONCE WE HIT FORTY,

women have only about four
taste buds left: one for vodka,
one for wine, one for cheese and
one for chocolate.

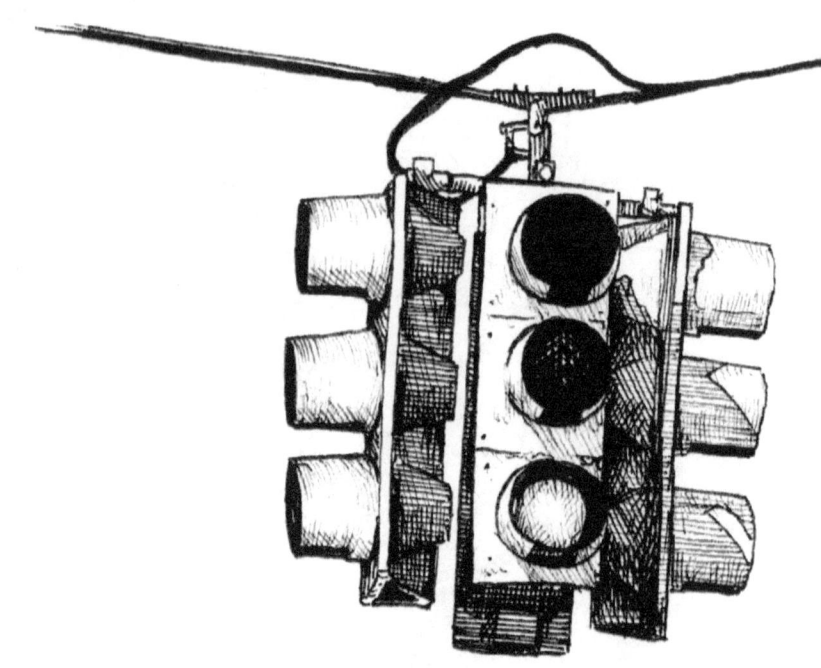

32

ONLY YES MEANS YES.

Want to know why we still ask for signatures on important documents or, for that matter, on receipts for items costing more than $49.99? Because active consent—even if it means a few extra steps—is worth it. Nobody should enter into an alliance (whether brief and superficial or life-changing and eternal) with a recalcitrant partner.

TO GET TO CONTENTMENT,

you probably need to go straight through heartbreak, then make a sharp turn.

34

YOU'RE NOT NUTS

and you're not alone.
Really.

YOU CANNOT
COUNT ON

35

the praise of others to keep you going. Ever. You will almost never get it and when you do get it, you won't get enough of it. And when you do get it, it won't be the right kind. Also, it probably won't be the right person saying it. Or it won't be about the right thing. It doesn't work that way. Learn to give yourself credit.

THERE ARE FEW THINGS WORSE

36

than feeling like an
embarrassment. Yet that's
how I've felt for much of my
life: I tag along, uninvited,
unchosen, annoying, as if my
presence must be accompanied
by a shrugged explanation or a
shushed apology.

The fear? I'm there as a default. They pretend to accept

me because they're too embarrassed to admit they've abandoned me, ditched me by the side of the road. Don't assume outward confidence indicates inner self-esteem.

37
CHAOS

in our lives is unfailing; tomorrow is
promised to no one. Is it a surprise, then, that
we embrace humor? When you can't count
on being happy or being loved, at least you
can count on being able to amuse yourself.

EVERYBODY ELSE'S PAIN

is easy to take. You can put it all into
perspective. Broken heart? At least it's
not a broken leg. Broken leg? At least it's
not a broken heart. Bad cold? Better than
pneumonia. Pneumonia? Better than
depression. Evicted? At least you still have
your car. Car repossessed? At least you
don't have to worry quite so much about
your broken heart. You need to worry
about finding a ride.

38

39

"USE AS DIRECTED"

does not apply to life.
Change directions. Do
what is not in the script.

DON'T LET YOURSELF GET OVERWHELMED BY "ACHIEVEMENT DYSMORPHIA".

"Achievement Dysmorphia" is the sense of disconnection women experience when our manifest accomplishments do not align with our unshakeable and inveterate sense of unworthiness. It's neither healthy nor charming. It's time for us to stop rehearsing our shortcomings. When they are due, we should accept congratulations with grace and pleasure—right along with the other responsibilities of success.

10

41 FROM THE TIME OF THE TROGLODYTES

women understood that we could not
compete with men through brute strength.
So we developed strategies to harness our
powerlessness to the point where, paradoxically,
it's been used as effective instrument of power.

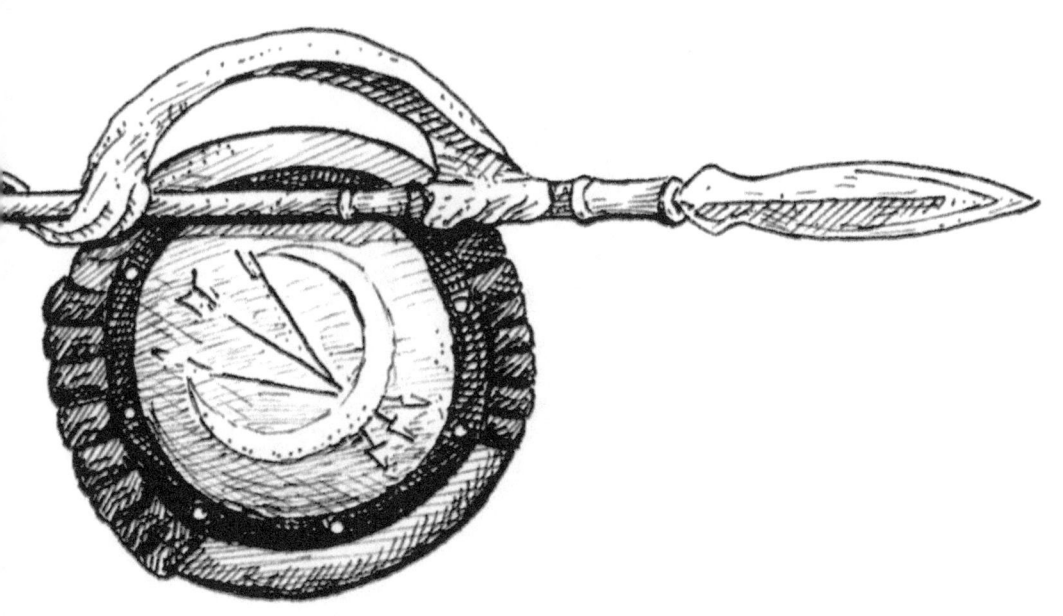

Historically, damp eyelashes and a wistful smile have achieved more for women than a display of anger or a show of authority.

Let's change that, shall we?

YOU CAN'T FIX EVERYTHING.

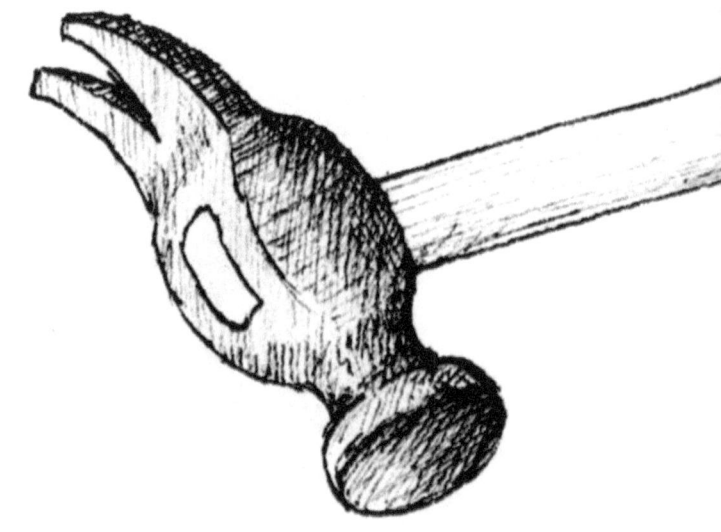

Some things can't be fixed, and fate is
rarely fair. Life is great, not easy.

42

43 A PERSON CAN BE

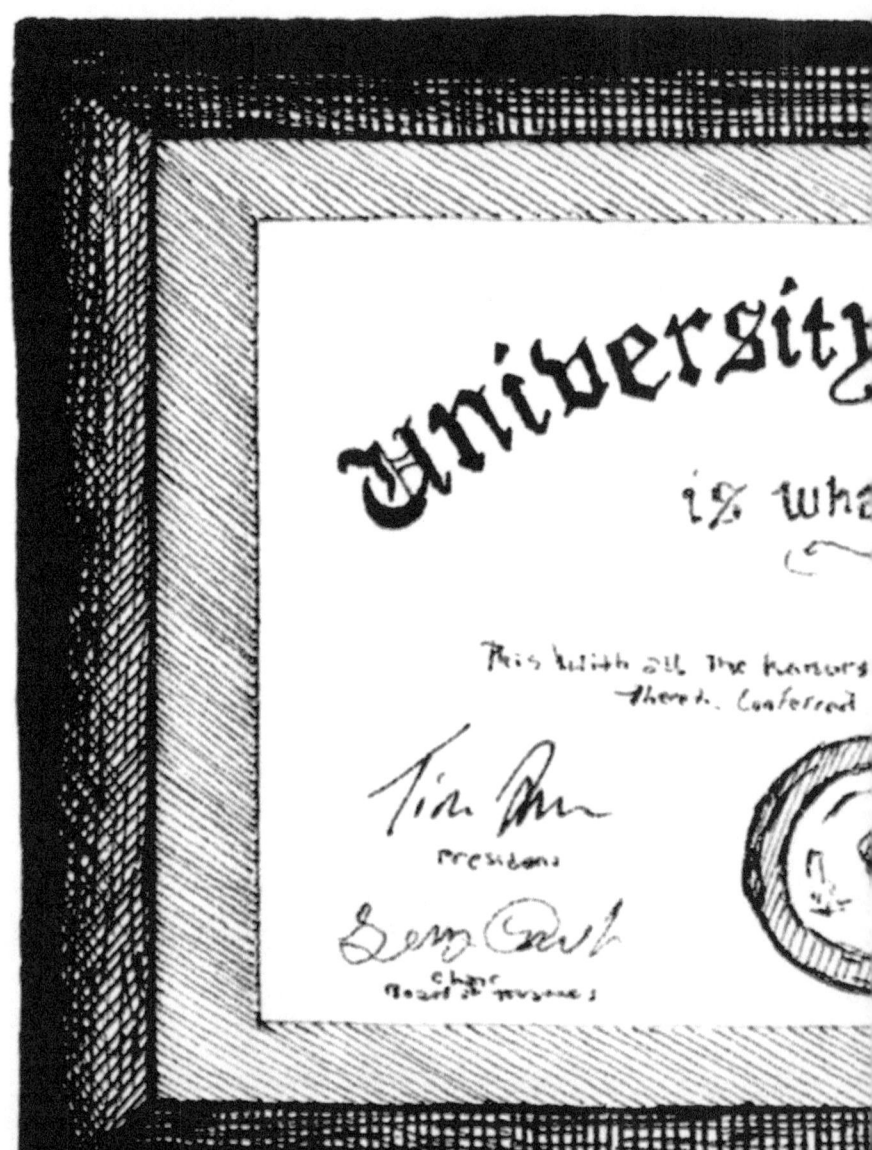

ridiculously well-schooled and yet startlingly stupid. You can also be dazzlingly smart and have dropped out of school after the fifth grade.

YOU ARE
GROWN-UP

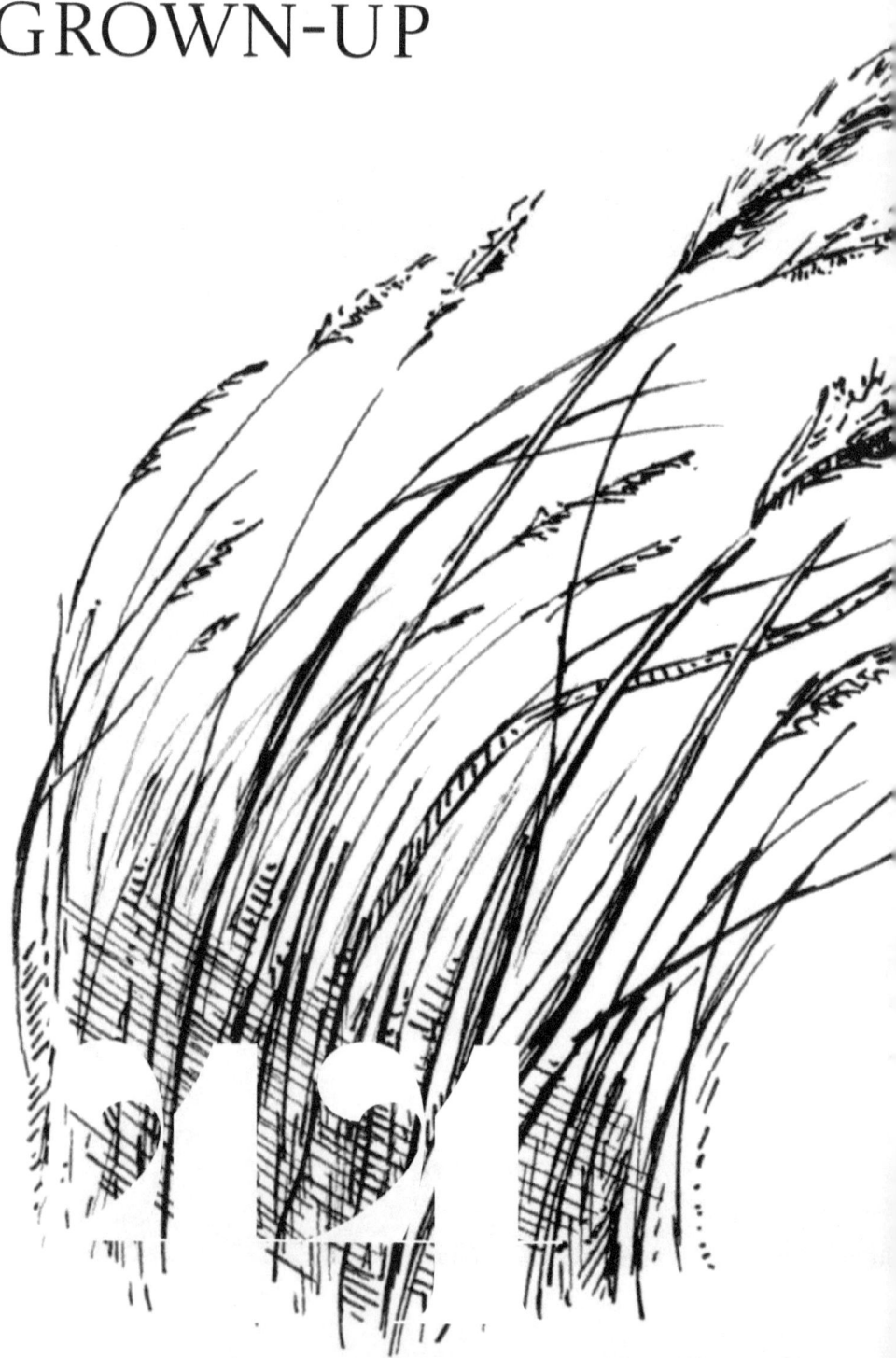

when you have the courage to face THE
ONE person in the world you CAN'T bear
to face, and you just do it, and let it go.

"WHERE'S THE RESTROOM?"

& "Do you love me?" deserve
immediate responses. Few others do.

I WILL COUNT MY BLESSINGS

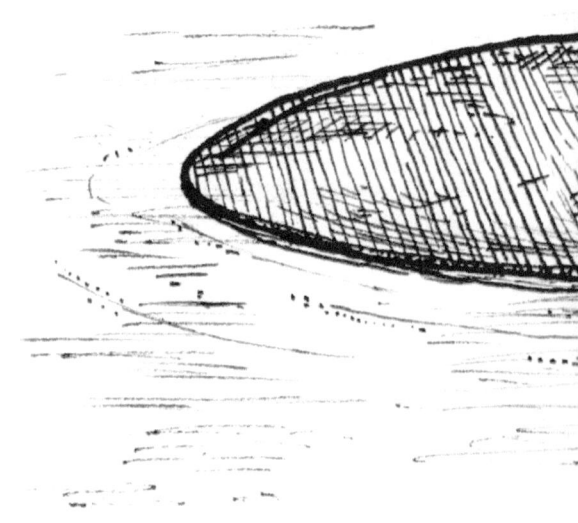

46

when I am in the doldrums, count to 10
when I am quarrelsome, and count on
my friends when I need a laugh.

NOBODY

is older than Norma Desmond.

48

MEN FEAR

that women use tears to control others. But when women DO give into tears, it's because we've LOST control and are more enraged than saddened. The image of the weeping woman in film, on television, or in any kind of theatrical representation whatsoever, including needlepoint and picture postcards has, in fact, done a great deal of harm to real women who are driven TO actual tears. That's because portrayals of women weeping are all wistful and attractive, whereas actual women who cry look heartbreaking and a teensy bit scary. Instead of impossibly attractive, lip-quivering Julie Christie or Scarlett Johansson, we make spectacles of ourselves. We make loud walrus-like noises when we sob, our mascara runs, our eyes puff up like portobello mushrooms, and we get splotchy.

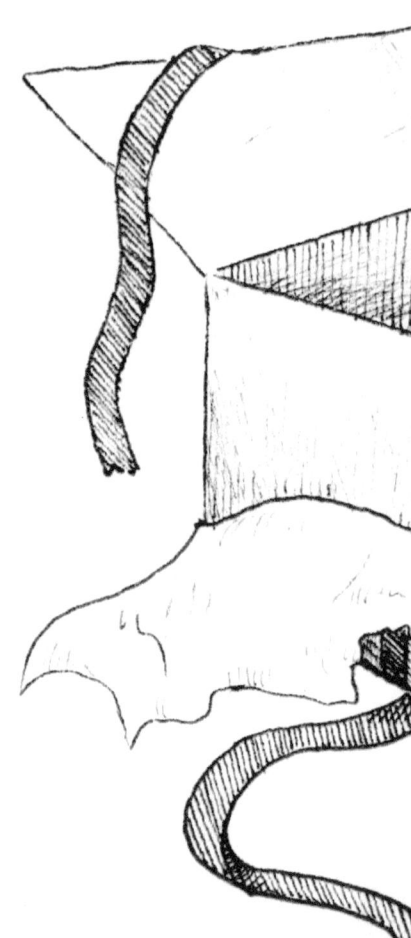

DON'T SIGH

over the golden days of yore. (My father
would have said "The golden days of your
what?") Leave the past to the past. Celebrate
the here and the now. Open the present.

49

50

IF YOU
THINK

of The Supreme Being as a rich
but distant relative who needs
placating in case He might leave
you something (or do you a good
turn in the future) you might want
to examine the role of faith in your
life. And the role of bribes.

THE PREMISE...

...behind shapewear is
this: if you put Jell-O
into a thermos, it won't
remember it's Jell-O.

THE UNEXAMINED LIFE

is not worth living.
But there are limits.

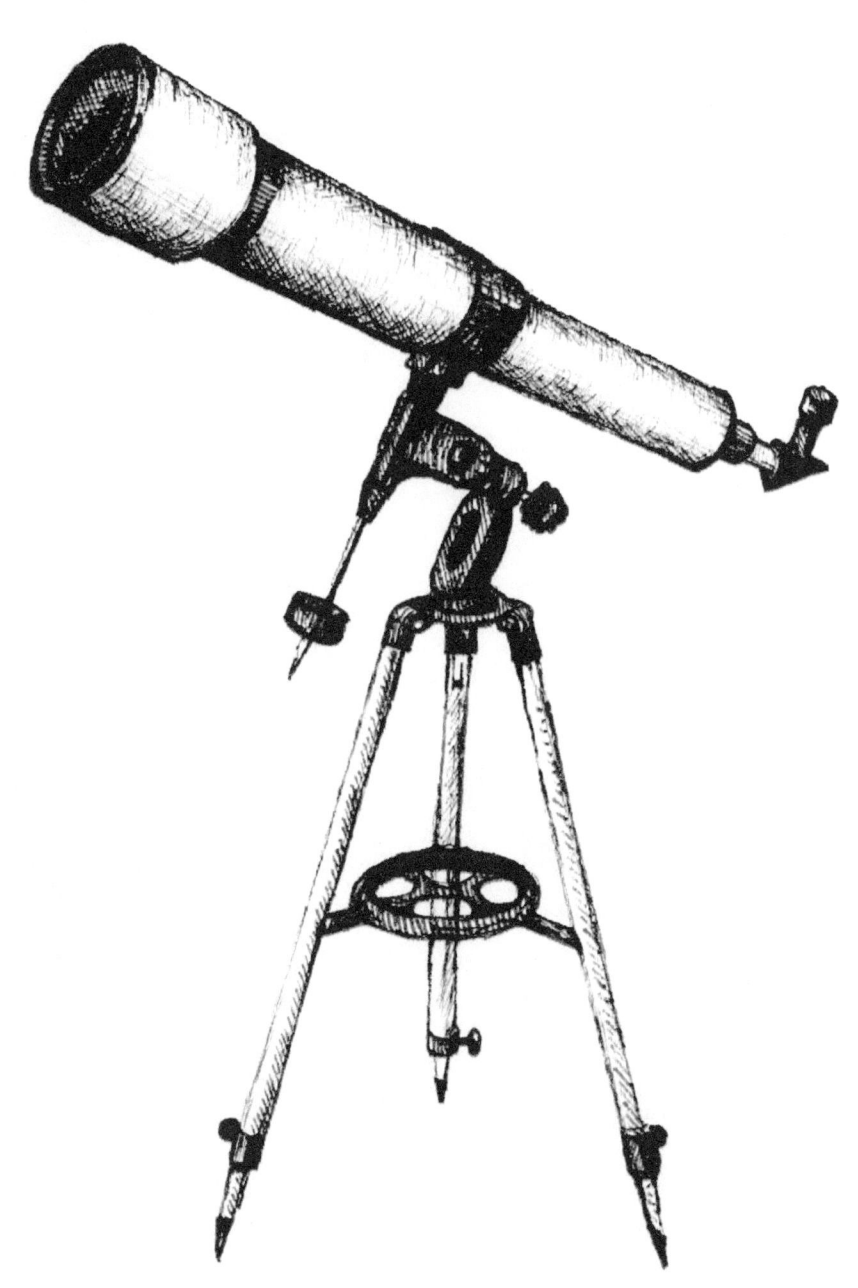

ASKING "DO YOU

remember what you said to
me a long time ago that still
genuinely hurts my feelings?"
will probably not end in a
hug and kiss.

I WILL STOP COLLECTING

old grievances as if they were old perfume
bottles or weirdly distorted Hummel figures.
I will get over being indignant and I will
shrug off being huffy. Impatience takes too
much time, unfunny bitterness ruins the
flavor of life, and resentment gives me lines
that make my mouth go down at the edges,
which is not a good look.

54

LIFE

infused with courage doesn't rule
out life laced with fear. Brave and
scared walk arm-in-arm.

YOUR FAVORITE SONG

might be one you haven't heard
yet. Here's to hope.

YOU AGE

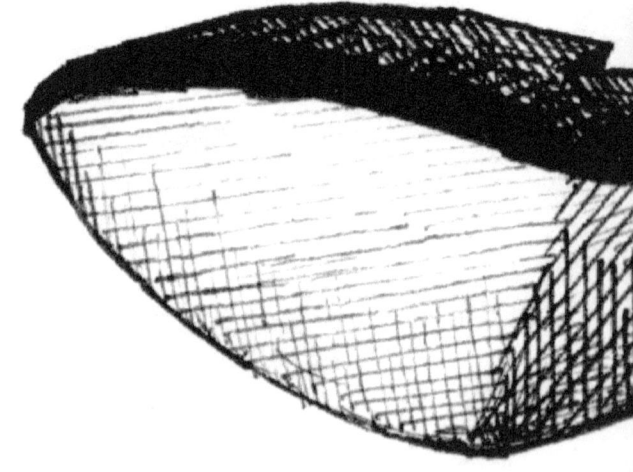

all at once. Nobody ages gradually.
One day you look at yourself and—
whoa.

57

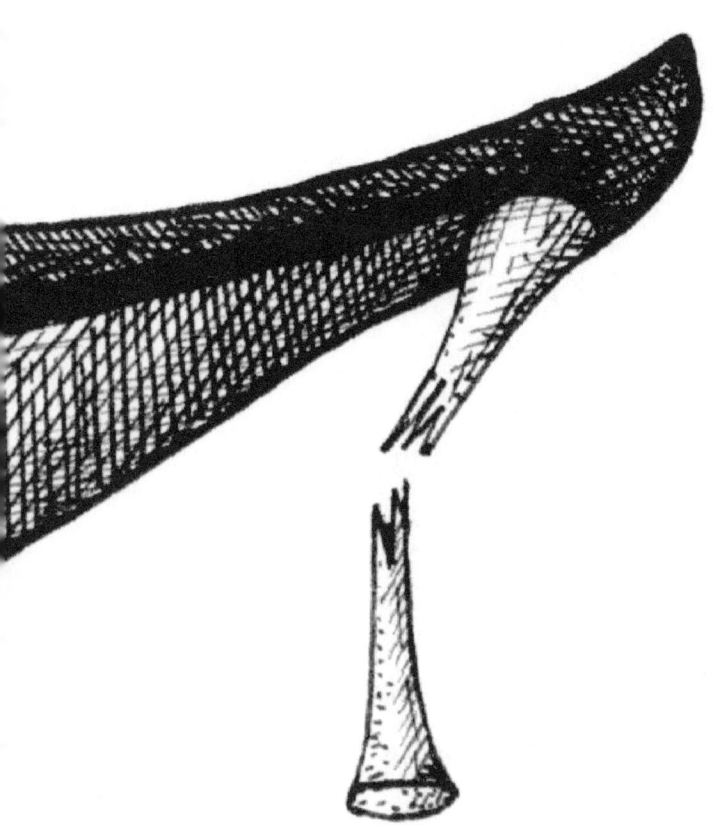

ANYONE WHO

lives in the mistaken belief that muttering, "I probably shouldn't even be telling you this" will bring you closer to them has made a perilous choice.

You are the one they put in danger; they remain in control of the situation.

If someone "shouldn't be telling you this"—if they are betraying someone else's confidence by saying it and if the information only serves to make them feel important because they think they have a secret—then the warning is right. This is not something you should hear.

58

EVEN DURING
THOSE
MOMENTS

when we're feeling desperately,
despairingly alone, we are kind of
kidding ourselves—if only we could
see it. Looking around, we could at
any moment encounter forty million
other desperately alienated outsiders
chanting exactly the same ode of
dejection. We're like a conga-line of
the Alienated Outsiders.

HUMOR

is a show of both strength and
vulnerability: you are willing to make
the first move, but you are trusting in the
response of your listener.

THE PHRASE "DYSFUNCTIONAL FAMILY"

is redundant. Nobody's home life is uncomplicated; few childhoods are easy. That's why adults weep while reading children's books. I can't even finish "Goodnight Moon" because by the time we say goodnight to the fire-escape or whatever the hell else we're leaving behind, I'm sobbing uncontrollably.

in myself and in others a ferocious
hunger for learning and an unquenchable
need to be generous; I will celebrate
whenever possible, reassure whenever
necessary, and prevail even if it means
being called "bitchy."

I WILL ENCOURAGE

62

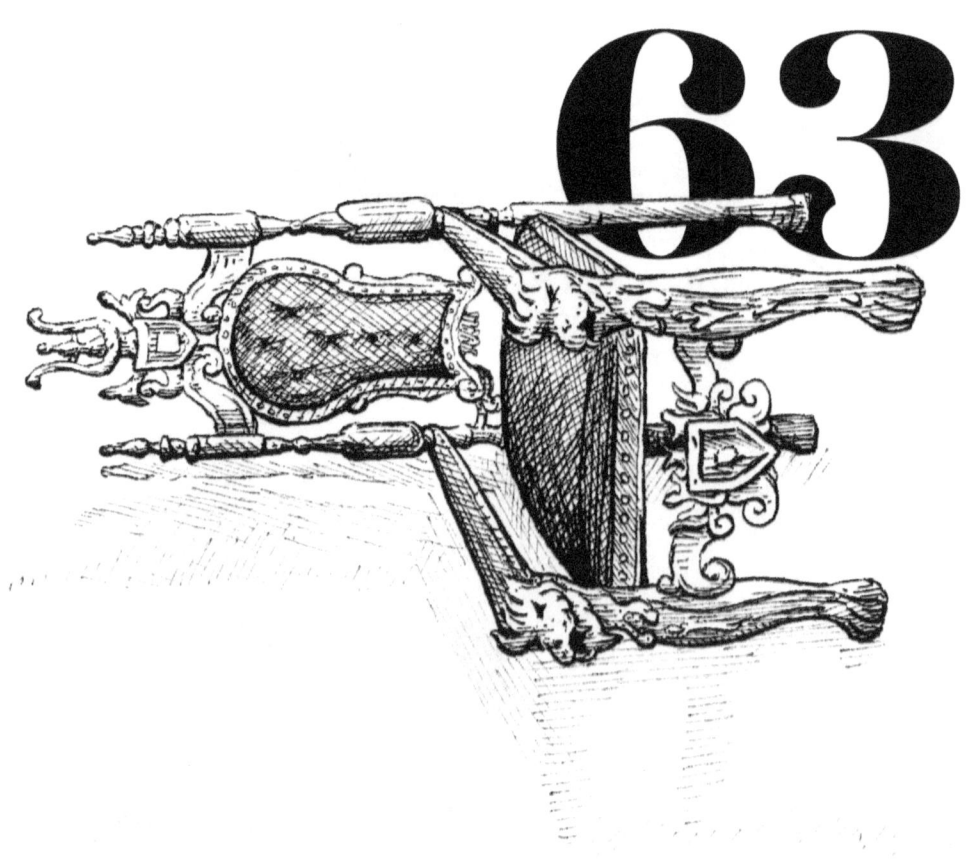

63

EVERY TIME A WOMAN

opens her mouth and
says something funny, she
makes trouble.

6⁴

IF EVE

had two daughters and not two
sons, would one have killed the
other? I don't think so.

EDUCATION

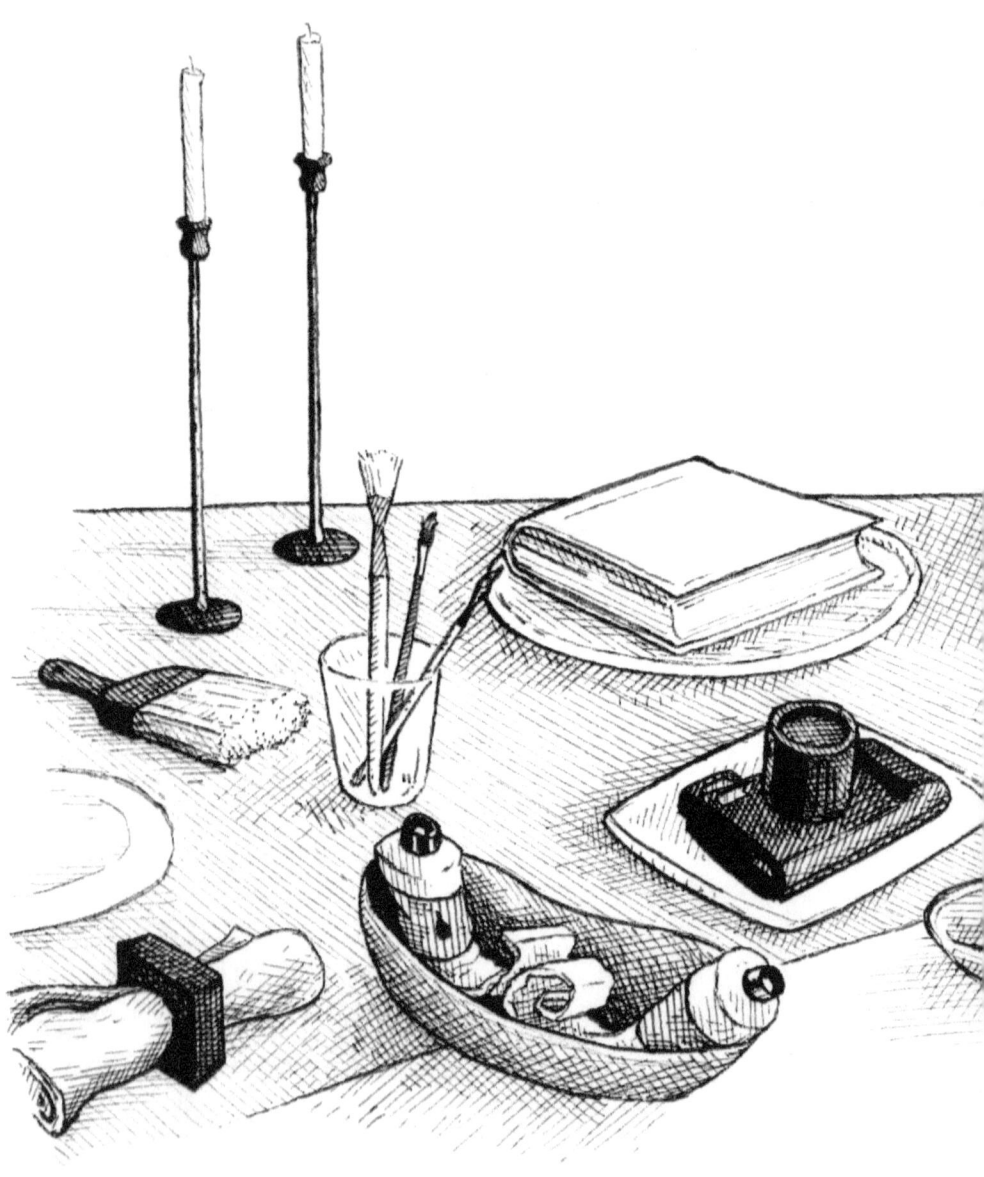

is like an all-you-can-learn buffet that's open
24-hours for a person's entire life.

65

MY
FEARS

36

taught me that even if they
can't be entirely overcome,
they can be faced and
sometimes outwitted.

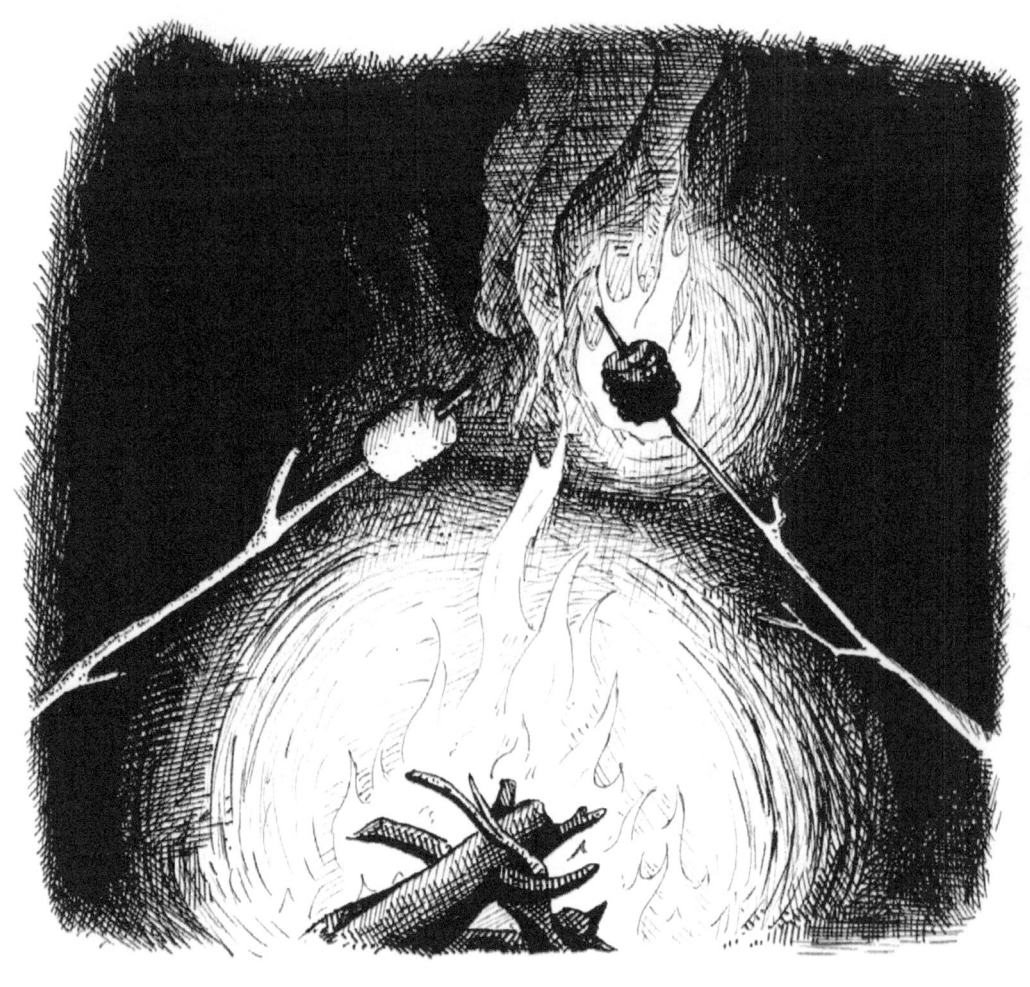

IF
SOMEONE

wide-eyed asks, "Are you mad at me?" you must instantly ask yourself, "Why is this person mad AT ME?" Then back away slowly as you figure out the answer.

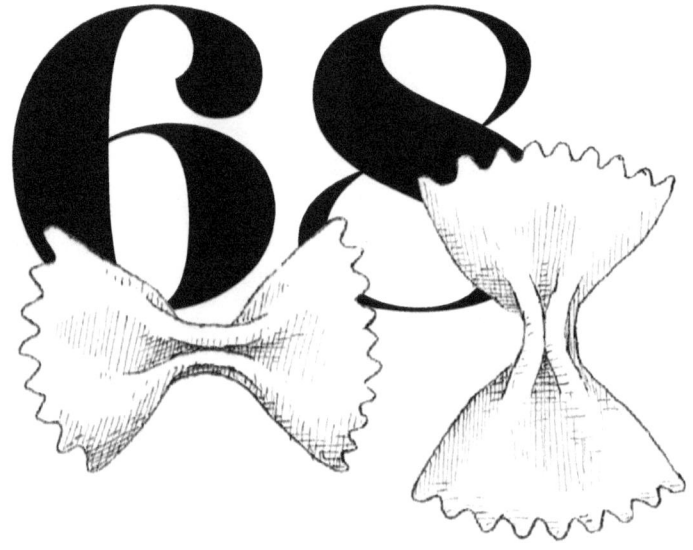

SOME
THINGS

are simply better the second
time around. These include
pasta, turkey, and love.
Help yourself.

DON'T TAKE PIECES

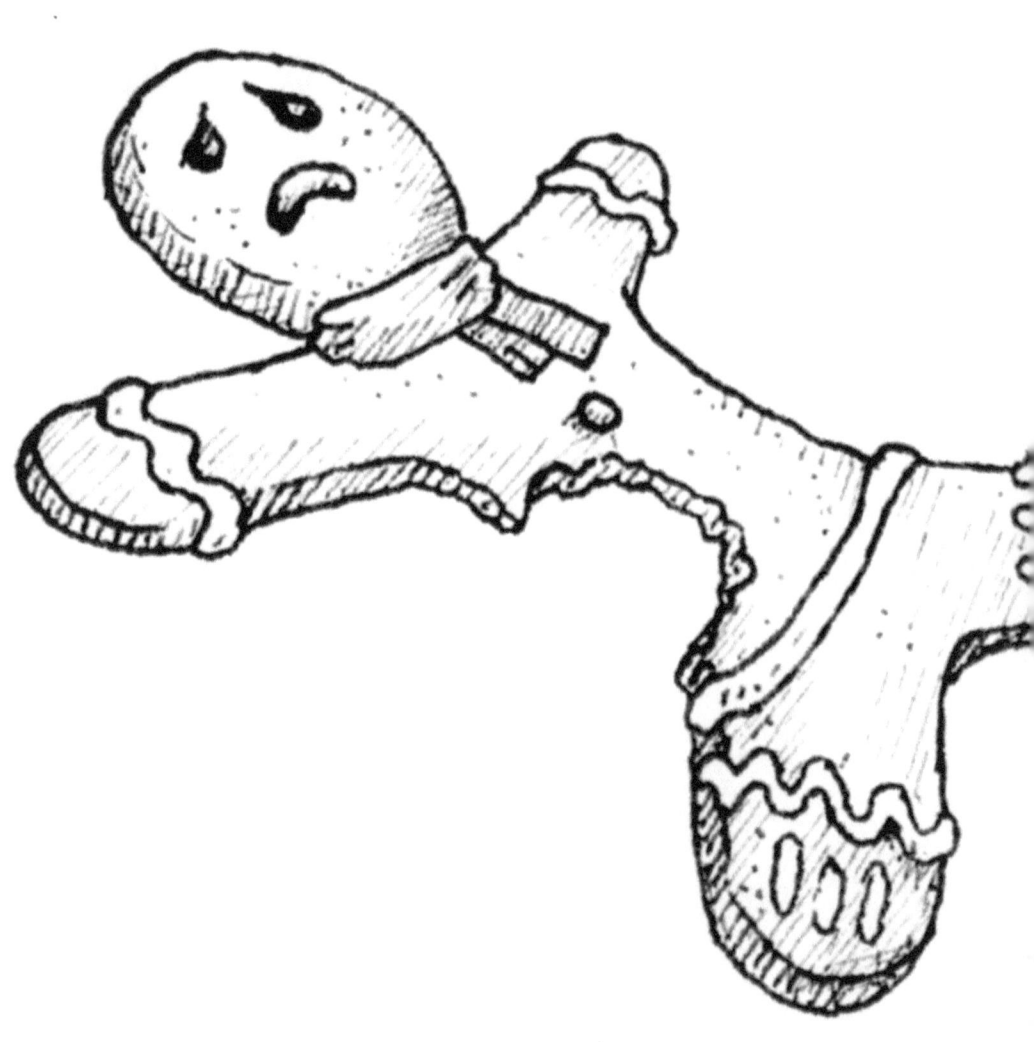

out of yourself to make others
happy; real friends don't
devour.

69

WE CAN

forgo festivities if we choose; we have
permission to wave good-bye to rituals
that no longer meet our needs. I can send
you a note with these words on it if you
need to carry a reminder, or to act as a
talisman to ward off guilt.

70

THERE'S

no real harm in revisiting the past as long as you remember you're only passing through.

71

72

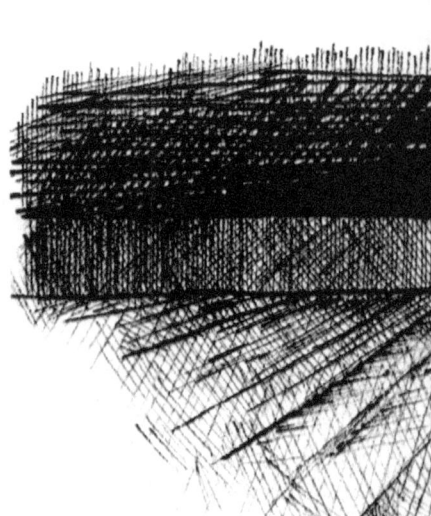

The one person from whom these purportedly valuable items remain hidden is me: I can never remember where I put something after I put it away for safekeeping.

I WILL STOP
HIDING THINGS
TO KEEP THEM
SAFE.

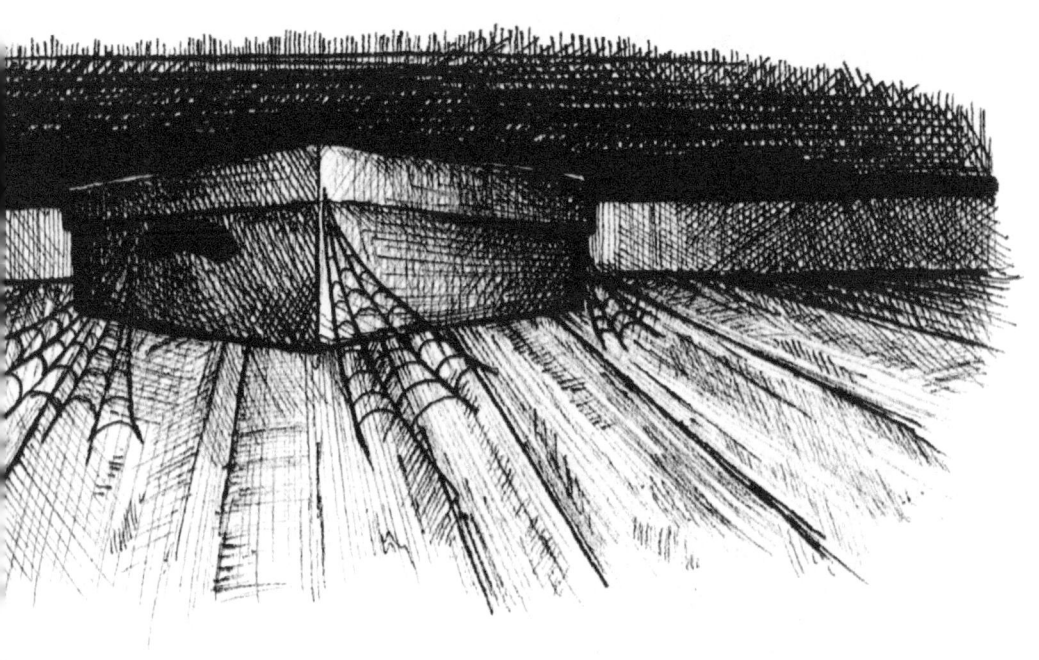

SOME
MISTAKES

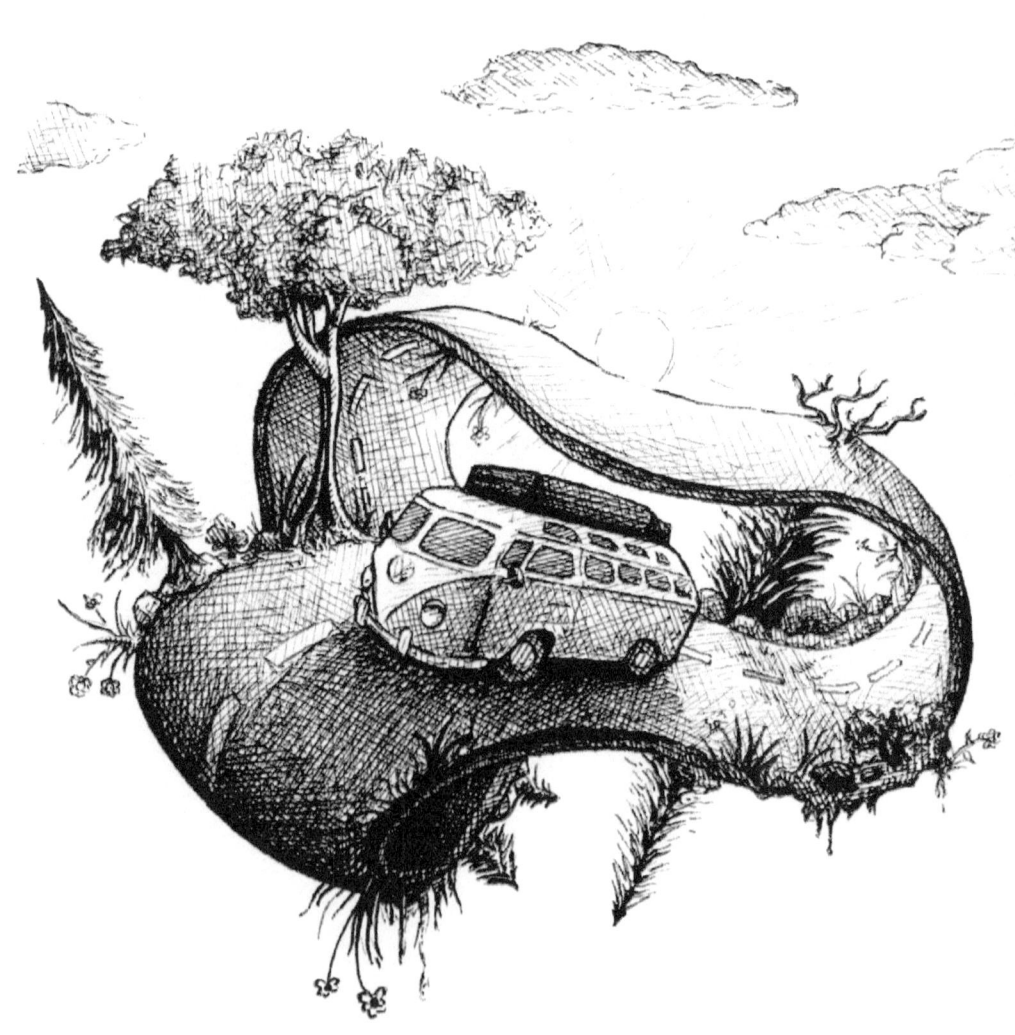

are worth repeating.

74

HUMOR

is our culture's third rail.
It's electrified, powerful,
and dangerous.

ANYBODY WITH A REAL MIND

is very nearly
always out of it.

76

TIME STRAINS
AT THE LEASH.

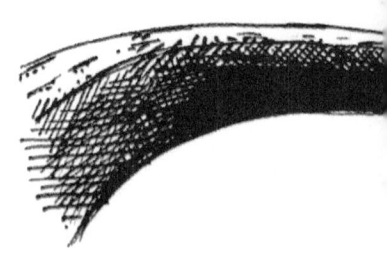

I can't control it. It runs, sits, rolls
over, then lunges baring teeth.
Unpredictable.

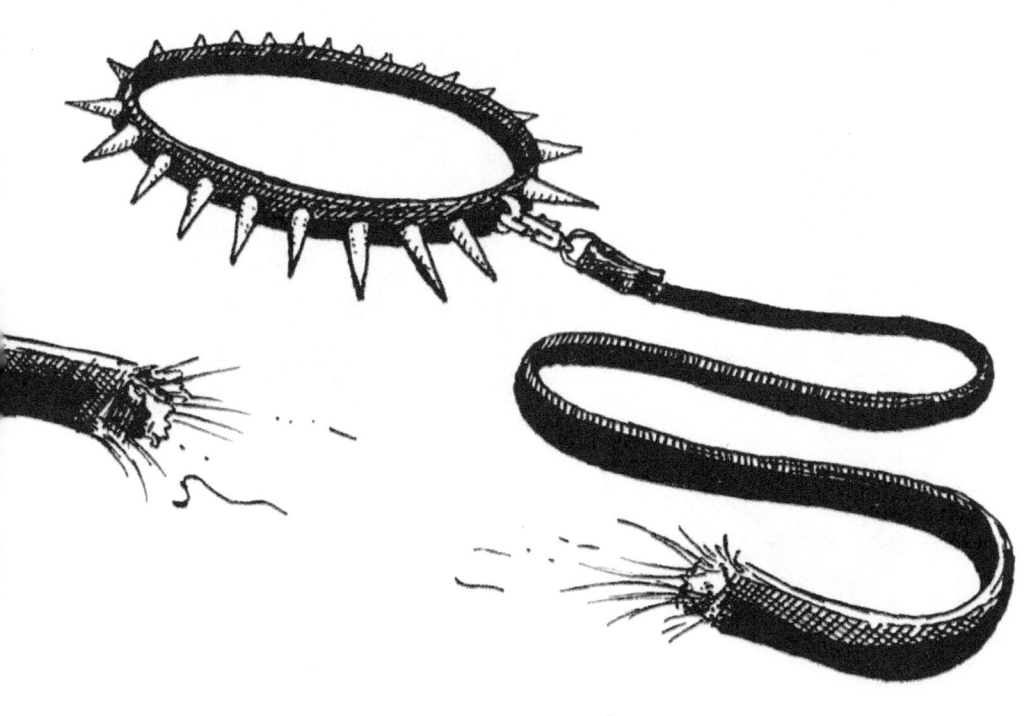

THERE
ARE DAYS

when you realize there is no change in
your circumstances, but you're restless,
antsy. It's like having a bad-hair-day
but internally.

78

WHEN
PRESENTED
WITH FREEDOM
OF CHOICE,

most of us would
prefer not to have to
make a decision.

79

A BAD
PARENT

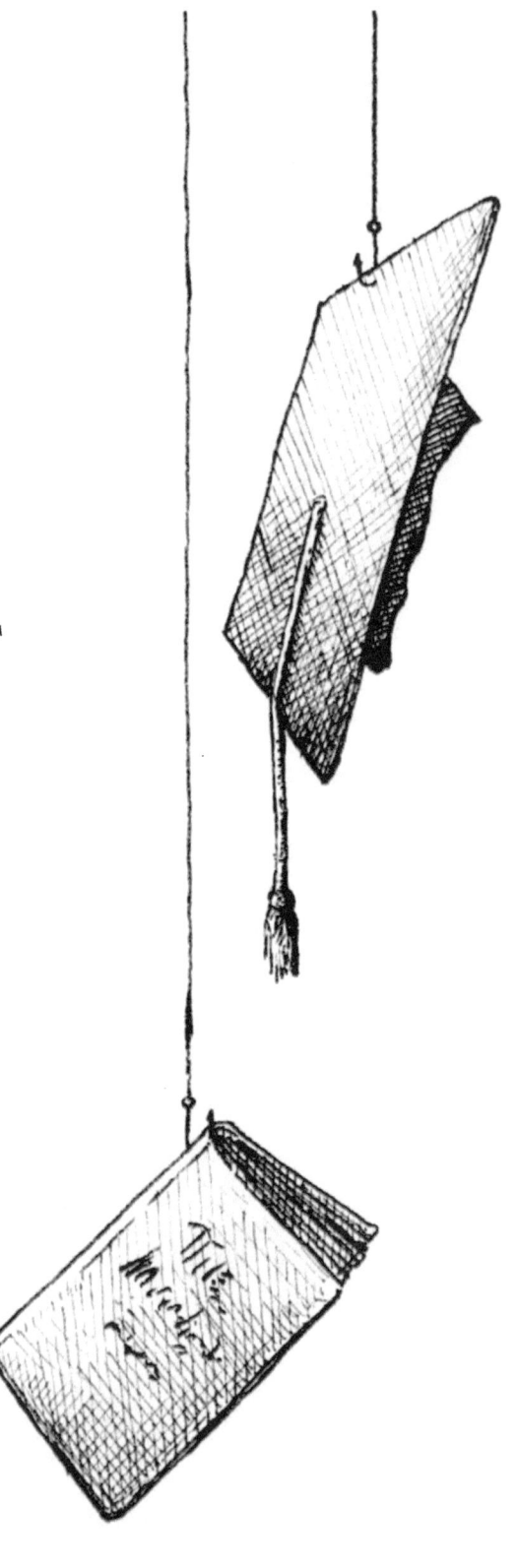

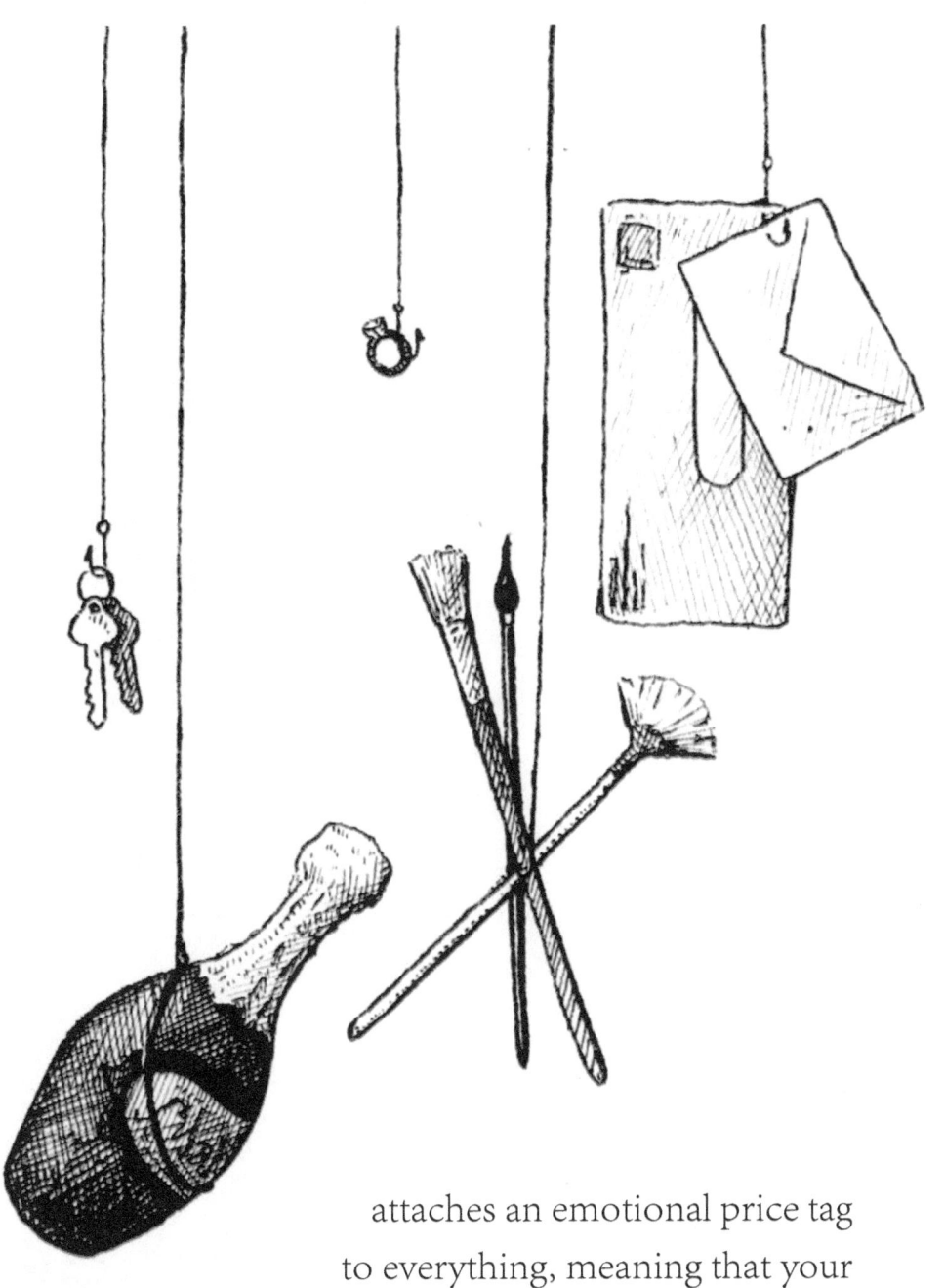

attaches an emotional price tag
to everything, meaning that your
success is their success, your failure is their failure
and, essentially, nothing is ever yours. They're not
there as a support or a guide but as an overseer
and a judge.

WHEN
I HIT 14
BACK IN
1971,

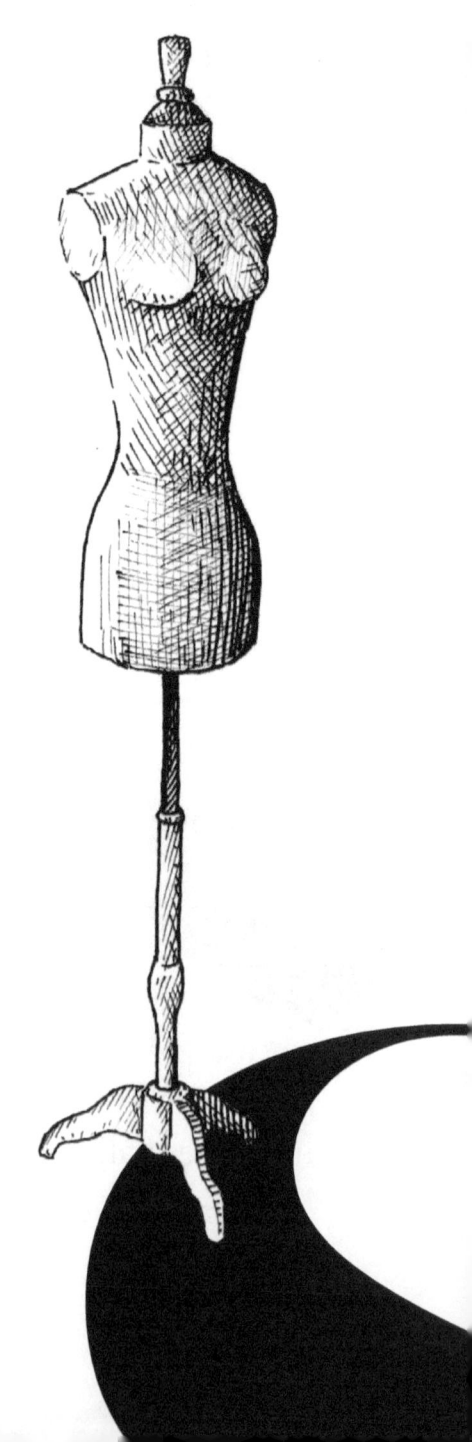

my mom told me I should start thinking about marriage because a husband would offer me support, like an underwire. A husband would keep me in control, like a girdle. A husband would help disguise my imperfections, like a slip. Men, from my mother's perspective, were basically one big foundation garment: once your secondary sex characteristics were apparent, they were essential. You wouldn't want to be seen on the street without one.

81

IF IT
WEREN'T
FOR OUR
RELATIVES,

we might never have to
be in the company of
people we didn't like.

AS I ALWAYS SAY,

Lorelei Lee got it wrong in "Gentlemen Prefer Blondes": It's not that diamonds are a girl's best friend, but it's your best friends who are your diamonds. It's your best friends who are supremely resilient, made under pressure, and of astonishing value. They're everlasting, and they can cut glass if they need to.

FOR THE WOMAN

who wakes up in the middle of the night wondering how to do it better next time...

For the woman who spills out, spills over, overdoes it, and can't contain herself...

For the one who knows it isn't perfect, thinks she should have started sooner, and knows that even if the world isn't paying attention, she is doing what she needs to have done...

Thank you.

83

LAUGHTER

84

is as close as
you can get to
a hug without
touching.

WE INSIST

on believing that a flat tummy,
toned arms, thin thighs, and a firm
neck will make us feel better about
ourselves when all it actually takes
to feel better is a martini and a
plate of cheese snacks.

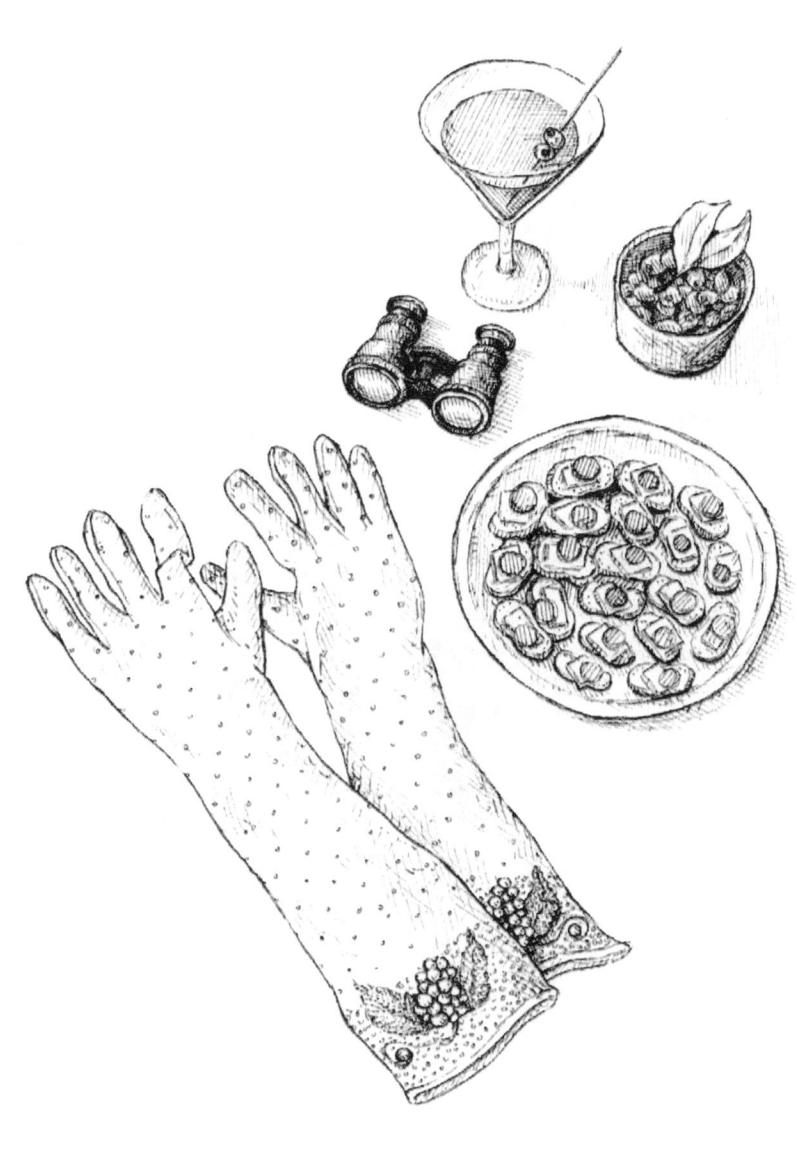

THE SECRET IS THERE IS NO SECRET.

80

In Heaven, no one brings out a list and asks you to say "sorry" for all the bad you've done. Rather, they ask you to explain why you did not accept all the opportunities you were given to embrace joy.

I WASTE A LOT OF TIME

wishing I had
more time.

88

TURNING
ANXIETY INTO
HUMOR

is the equivalent
of spinning straw
into gold.

BIG
THINGS

happen when you're not expecting them,
when you're not looking. It happens in
history and it happens in life. One morning
there was moveable type. One morning there
was chloroform for operations... And one
morning you wake up and you're in love,
or you're breaking up with the person you
once adored, or you've won an award for the
work you've loved doing. One morning you
wake up and nothing is ever the same again.

NO
STRAIGHT
MAN

in Western Civilization has ever
tried on a bathing suit. Men wear the
bathing suit their mothers bought them
when they were seventeen until there's
a hole where they put their keys, and
then they walk into some cheap store,
find the sale bin, find a suit, hold it up,
say, "It's blue; it'll fit," and they leave.

91

A WOMAN WITH
A GOOD FATHER

is an heiress.

TELL YOUR FRIGHTENED OR DESPAIRING YOUNGER SELF

that she can borrow your courage. Tell your
worried or bereft older self that she, too,
can draw on your account. When times are
tough, we can lend ourselves strength.

92

When you're anxious, worried,
or scared, you realize it isn't
sense you're looking for.

PEOPLE HAVE TALKED
SENSE TO ME.

What I want, I can't have.
I can only have what I don't want.
To get something, I must not want it.

94

WROTE THIS AS A TEENAGER.

Spent most of my
life trying not to
believe it.

95

IT'S COMPLICATED

to be in a relationship
with somebody you
don't trust, especially if
that somebody is your
parent. Or your spouse.
Or yourself.

YOU EARN
YOUR COURAGE,

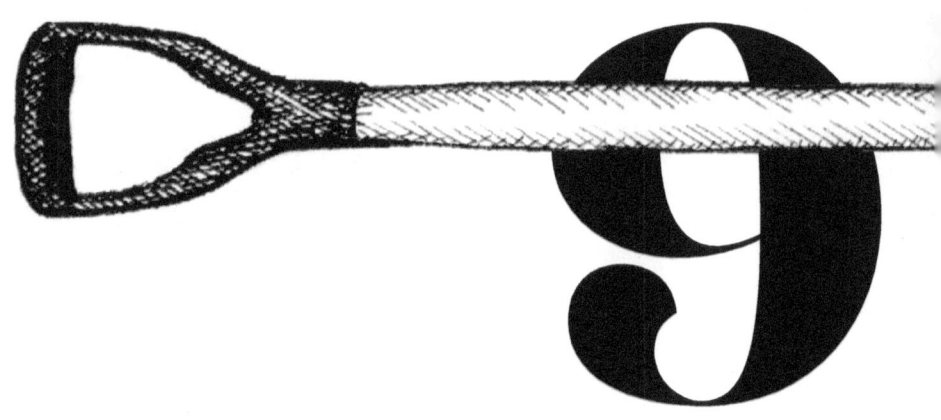

9

you build on your courage, and,
when necessary, you can draw
on your courage. You probably
have more than you realize. Use
it; don't hide it, hide behind it,
or allow it to be buried with you.
You're braver than you think.

KEEP A SENSE OF HUMOR
ON YOU AT ALL TIMES.

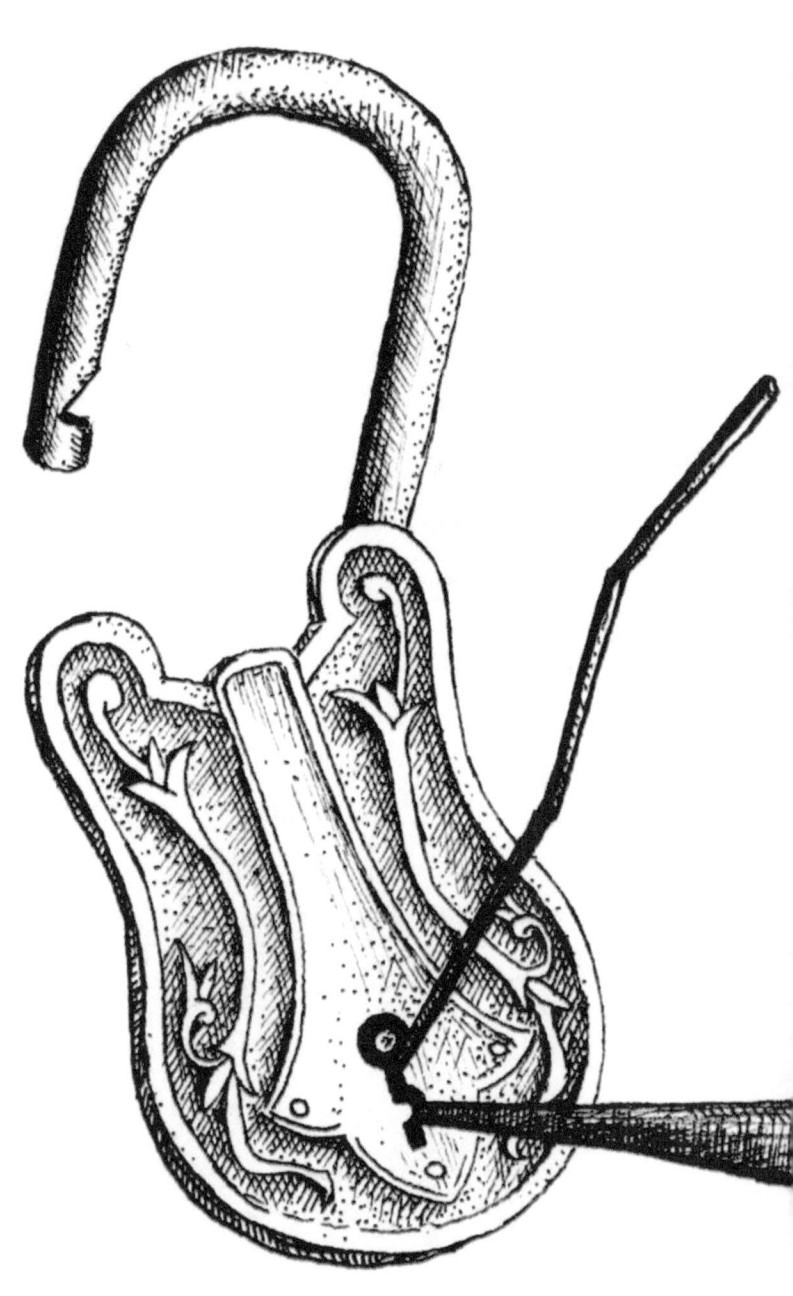

97

Using humor leads to recuperation, restoration, and redemption; often the worst moments can transform themselves into the funniest stories. Humor allows you to get your spiritual deposit back from periods of tragedy, betrayal, loss, and fear. It is emotional recycling at its best. Once you make an event into a story, it's no longer just something that happened to you. You control it. If you hone it to a fine point, humor can be the instrument you use to pick the lock of pretty much anything that's trying to keep you out.

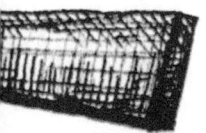

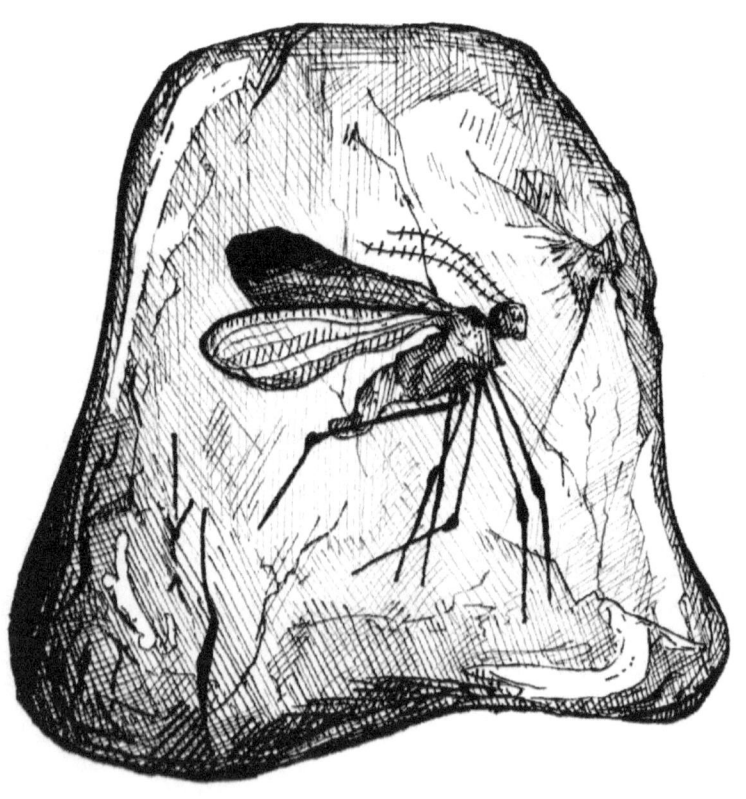

I'M NOT
A FAN

of products promoted as
"anti-aging." The opposite of
aging isn't staying young. The
opposite of aging is death.

LIFE ITSELF
IS A GROUP
PROJECT:

 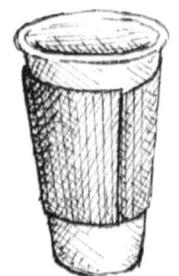

we've all got a deadline. We have to
forgive those who let us down the
way we hope to be forgiven by those
we've disappointed.

THE
INTENSITY

100

of an emotion
does not imply the
durability of that
emotion.

101

IN DECIDING

what to do next,
examine what came before you.

10

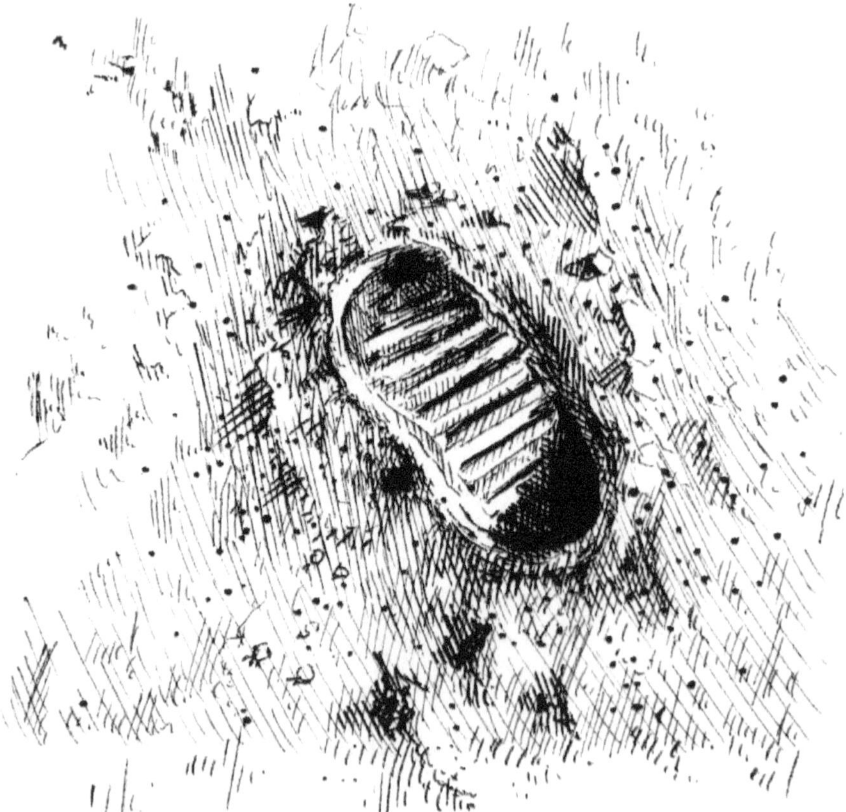

STOP ALREADY

with platform sandals. Summer sandals should, by definition, be easy-going comfy shoes. Platforms, by definition, are a weird scaffolding you put on your feet. They confuse your body. Your body wonders "Are we having fun now, or are we going for a walk on the moon?"

DECIDE WHAT'S WORTH YOUR EFFORT,

loyalty, and time. Take your
hands away from your eyes and
you might be dazzled.

ABOUT THE AUTHOR

Dr. Gina Barreca is the author of ten books, including the bestselling *They Used to Call Me Snow White but I Drifted* as well as *Babes in Boyland: A Personal History of Coeducation in the Ivy League*, and *It's Not That I'm Bitter, or How I learned to Stop Wearing Visible Pantylines and Conquered the World*. Board of Trustees Distinguished Professor of English Literature at the University of Connecticut, you've seen her on PBS's *American Masters*, heard her on NPR's *This American Life*, and delighted in the advice she's dispensed on *The TODAY Show*, CNN, the BBC, *Entertainment Tonight*, *48 Hours*, and during several appearances on *Oprah*. You've read her in the *New York Times*, *The Chicago Tribune*, *Cosmopolitan*, *Forbes*, *The Chronicle of Higher Education*, *The Harvard Business Review*, and *Psychology Today;* for fifteen years, she wrote a weekly column distributed by the McClatchy/Tribune syndicate and published worldwide. An expert on humor, Gina has delivered keynotes at more than 500 events, including ones held by The Smithsonian, The Erma Bombeck Writers Workshop, the National Writers Workshop, the Chicago Humanities Festival, and Women in Federal Law Enforcement. Gina's degrees are from Dartmouth College, The Graduate Center of CUNY, and Cambridge University. Growing up in Brooklyn and Long Island, she now lives with her husband in Storrs, CT. She can be found in the Library of Congress or the make-up aisle of Walgreens. Feel free to ask her advice about concealer.

www.ginabarreca.com

ABOUT THE ARTIST

John Guillemette is a writer and artist who enjoys hikes, houseplants, and disparaging mankind. He reads monks and drunks; if a monk wrote it, or a drunk wrote it, then he's probably read it. His satire has appeared in *Little Old Lady Comedy*, and his stories have been published in *The Wild Word, Book of Matches,* and *Long River Review*, where he received the Edwin Way Teale Award for nature writing. He lives in New Haven, CT.

www.musingjohn.com

ACKNOWLEDGMENTS

Gina Barreca

Without Dave LeGere of Woodhall, once an undergraduate student in my creative writing course at the University of Connecticut, there would be no *GINA SCHOOL*. Dave's dynamic imagination helped me realize what this small, beautiful book could be. John Guillemette, another former student with artistic talents and skills, insight and intelligence, made it happen. Their enthusiasm, patience, and perspicacity brought me joy as we made creative decisions together.

So that the acknowledgements won't have more words than the book itself, here's a gathering of those to whom I'm in the greatest debt and owe the wildest thanks: Alexander Grant, Amelia Sherman, Pamela Katz, Nancy B. Lager, Timothy W. Taylor, Hugo Barreca, Laura Rossi (great publicity!), Nancy LaFever (great copyediting!), as well as Miranda Heyman, Chris Madden, and Margaret Moore at Woodhall.

And yes, Michael, my husband, helped me learn about the good parts of love and the best parts of life. It's good to prepare for finals with somebody you trust.

ACKNOWLEDGMENTS

John Guillemette

I owe many thanks to my supportive family, especially my mom, Sara, who collected second-hand art supplies and befriended local artists so that my teenage self had access to mentorship and equipment on a budget. I'm also deeply grateful for Leeza Desjardins, my high school art teacher. Everything I got right—every well-placed line—was thanks to Mrs. D's excellent instruction. (As for the mistakes, those were all me.) Thank you, Josh, my unofficial brother and my strongest creative friendship, for all the late-night critiques and supportive words. My sincerest gratitude goes out to Dr. Joel Dodson, Rachel Furey, Charles Baraw, and Timothy Parrish for mentoring me throughout my creative professionalism. Special thanks to Dave, Miranda, Chris, and Margaret of Woodhall Press, for keeping us on-target, for spreading the word, and for matching our enthusiasm for the project. And, though it nearly goes without saying, many, many thanks to Gina Barreca for writing such compelling words (I had so much fun visually interpreting them!) and for thinking of me when it came time to find a collaborator.